Blueprints Q&A
STEP 2: MEDICINE

Blueprints Q&A
STEP 2: MEDICINE

SERIES EDITOR:
Michael S. Clement, MD

Fellow, American Academy of Pediatrics
Mountain Park Health Center
Phoenix, Arizona
Clinical Lecturer in Family
 and Community Medicine
University of Arizona College of Medicine
Consultant, Arizona Department
 of Health Services

EDITOR:
Gregory A. Maynard, MD, MS

Assistant Professor of Clinical Medicine,
 Department of Internal Medicine
University of Arizona College of Medicine
Senior Associate Program Director,
 Internal Medicine Residency
Good Samaritan Regional Medical Center
 Phoenix, Arizona

**Blackwell
Science**

EDITORIAL OFFICES:

Commerce Place, 350 Main Street,
    Malden, Massachusetts 02148, USA

Osney Mead, Oxford OX2 0EL, England

25 John Street, London WC1N 2BL, England

23 Ainslie Place, Edinburgh EH3 6AJ, Scotland

54 University Street, Carlton, Victoria 3053, Australia

OTHER EDITORIAL OFFICES:

Blackwell Wissenschafts-Verlag GmbH,
    Kurfürstendamm 57, 10707 Berlin, Germany

Blackwell Science KK, MG Kodenmacho Building,
    7-10 Kodenmacho Nihombashi, Chuo-ku,
    Tokyo 104, Japan

Iowa State University Press, A Blackwell Science Company,
    2121 S. State Avenue, Ames, Iowa 50014-8300, USA

DISTRIBUTORS:

The Americas
        Blackwell Publishing
        c/o AIDC
        P.O. Box 20
        50 Winter Sport Lane
        Williston, VT 05495-0020
        (Telephone orders: 800-216-2522;
        fax orders: 802-864-7626)

Australia   Blackwell Science Pty, Ltd.
        54 University Street
        Carlton, Victoria 3053
        (Telephone orders: 03-9347-0300;
        fax orders: 03-9349-3016)

Outside The Americas and Australia
        Blackwell Science, Ltd.
        c/o Marston Book Services, Ltd., P.O. Box 269
        Abingdon, Oxon OX14 4YN, England
        (Telephone orders: 44-01235-465500;
        fax orders: 44-01235-465555)

Figure credits: All photographs courtesy of Robert Raschke, MD, Good Samaritan Regional Medical Center/VA Internal Medicine Residency Program, Phoenix, Arizona

Acquisitions: Beverly Copland

Development: Angela Gagliano

Production: Irene Herlihy

Manufacturing: Lisa Flanagan

Marketing Manager: Toni Fournier

Cover design by Hannus Design

Typeset by Software Services

Printed and bound by Courier-Stoughton

Printed in the United States of America

01 02 03 04 5 4 3 2 1

Library of Congress Cataloging-in-Publication Data

Blueprints Q & A step 2. Medicine / editor,
Gregory A. Maynard.
        p. ; cm.—(Blueprints Q & A step 2 series)
    ISBN 0-632-04602-3 (pbk.)
    1. Medicine—Examinations, questions, etc.
    2. Physicians—Licenses—United States—Examinations—
    Study guides.
    [DNLM: 1. Clinical Medicine—Examination Questions.
WB 18.2 B658 2002] I. Title: Blueprints Q&A step 2.
Medicine. II. Title: Blueprints Q&A step 2. Medicine.
III. Title: Medicine. IV. Maynard, Gregory A. V. Title.
VI. Series.
    R834.5 .B58 2002
    616'.0076—dc21   2001002367

Notice: The indications and dosages of all drugs in this book have been recommended in the medical literature and conform to the practices of the general community. The medications described and treatment prescriptions suggested do not necessarily have specific approval by the Food and Drug Administration for use in the diseases and dosages for which they are recommended. The package insert for each drug should be consulted for use and dosage as approved by the FDA. Because standards for usage change, it is advisable to keep abreast of revised recommendations, particularly those concerning new drugs.

CONTRIBUTORS:

Jessica Spelman, MD
Chief Resident in Internal Medicine
Good Samaritan Regional Medical Center
Phoenix, Arizona

Born in Detroit, Michigan, Jessica grew up in the small town of Sunbury, Ohio. She attended the University of Toledo for undergraduate study, where she studied chemistry and biology. Jessica then received her medical degree in 1996 from The Ohio State University College of Medicine. Incredibly, 13 days after completing her combined residency in Internal Medicine and Pediatrics, Jessica became the proud new mother of her son Isaac.

Brenda Swander, MD
Chief Resident in Internal Medicine
Good Samaritan Regional Medical Center
Phoenix, Arizona

Like her identical twin sister, Brenda loves to teach. This has led to her decision to remain in academic medicine. Born in Indianapolis, Indiana, Brenda attended Grand Canyon University in Phoenix, Arizona, where she studied under a music scholarship for the violin. With concentrations in Biology and Chemistry, she then attended the University of Arizona, where she received her medical degree in 1997.

REVIEWERS:

Lynn Henry, MD

Class of 2001

Washington University

Saint Louis, Missouri

Intern

Brigham and Women's Hospital

Boston, Massachusetts

Lee Ann W. Koster, MD

Class of 2000

University of South Alabama College of Medicine

Mobile, Alabama

Resident in Emergency Medicine

University of Texas Southwestern at
    Parkland Hospital

Dallas, Texas

Uri Lopatin, MD

Class of 2000

University of Medicine and Dentistry of New Jersey -
    New Jersey Medical School Newark, New Jersey

Intern, Internal Medicine Program

University of Washington

Seattle, Washington

PREFACE

The Blueprints Q&A Step 2 series has been developed to complement our core content Blueprints books. Each Blueprints Q&A Step 2 book (*Medicine, Pediatrics, Surgery, Psychiatry,* and *Obstetrics/Gynecology*) was written by residents seeking to provide fourth-year medical students with the highest quality of practice USMLE questions.

Each book covers a single discipline, allowing you to use them during both rotation exams as well as for review prior to Boards. For each book, 100 review questions are presented that cover content typical to the Step 2 USMLE. The questions are divided into two groups of 50 in order to simulate the length of one block of questions on the exam.

Answers are found at the end of each book, with the correct option screened. Accompanying the correct answer is a discussion of why the other options are incorrect. This allows for even the wrong answers to provide you with a valuable learning experience.

Blackwell has been fortunate to work with expert editors and residents—people like you who have studied for and passed the Boards. They sought to provide you with the very best practice prior to taking the Boards.

We welcome feedback and suggestions you may have about this book or any in the Blueprints series. Send to blue@blacksci.com.

All of the authors and staff at Blackwell wish you well on the Boards and in your medical future.

ACKNOWLEDGMENTS

I would like to thank Dr. Brenda Swander and Dr. Jessica Spelman for their hard work and valuable input to all phases of this project. Kudos is also due to Dr. Bob Raschke for assisting us with his extensive medical image file. Lastly, sincere thanks to Dr. Alan Leibowitz, the program director of the GSRMC/Phoenix VAMC Internal Medicine Residency Program; without his generosity and flexibility, we could not have participated in this project.

Gregory A. Maynard

BLOCK **ONE**

QUESTIONS

QUESTION 1

A 36-year-old man presents to the ER with severe sudden onset chest discomfort. The pain is described as a ripping sensation that radiates to his back. His blood pressure is 170/70 in the left arm and 130/60 in the right arm. His pulse is 70 and regular, his respiratory rate is 20/min, and his height is 72 in. He weighs 160 lb. There is a soft diastolic decrescendo murmur over the left upper sternal border, no gallop, and clear lung fields. His EKG shows a sinus rhythm with non-specific ST-T changes. You note his unusual appearing hands and an abnormal chest x-ray as seen in the accompanying figures. What is the most likely source of his chest pain?

A. Acute myocardial infarction

B. Unstable angina

C. Aortic aneurysm dissection

D. Acute pulmonary embolus

E. Acute pericarditis

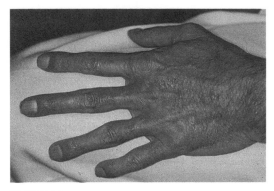

FIGURE 1A

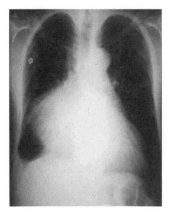

FIGURE 1B

QUESTION 2

A 25-year-old woman presents to your office with complaints of poor sleep, irritability, and nervousness. She appears anxious and restless. You note a resting tachycardia and a brawny edematous skin change on the dorsum of the lower legs and feet. She has striking eye and neck exam findings as shown in the accompanying figures. Which of the following findings should you expect on further evaluation?

A. A high free T_4 level

B. A low TSH level

C. Increased uptake on radioiodide nuclear thyroid scan

D. High levels of thyroid-stimulating antibodies

E. All of the above

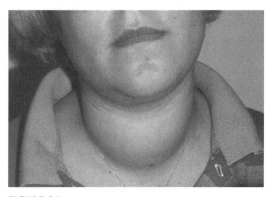

FIGURE 2A

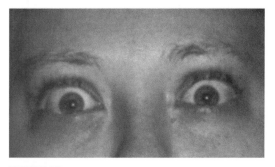

FIGURE 2B

QUESTION 3

A 58-year-old previously healthy white female presents with the complaint of chest pain and shortness of breath. The chest pain was of sudden onset, and it is mainly left-sided. She states that it is sharp in nature and worsens with inspiration. She denies cough, fevers, nausea, or palpitations. She smokes one pack of cigarettes per day. She takes no medications except hormone replacement and a multivitamin. On exam, she is afebrile with a blood pressure of 130/82, heart rate of 110/min, and respiratory rate of 26/min. Pulse oximetry shows oxygen saturation of 92% on room air. Her lungs are clear to auscultation, and she has no cardiac murmurs or jugular venous distension. EKG shows only sinus tachycardia, and a chest x-ray shows no infiltrate. Which of the following is the best next step in management?

A. Check serial CPKs with MB fraction

B. Cardiac catheterization and possible angioplasty

C. Begin coumadin

D. Ventilation-perfusion scan

E. Give TPA

QUESTION 4

A 56-year-old woman with a history of rheumatoid arthritis comes to the emergency department with complaints of abdominal pain that started abruptly in the last hour. She describes the pain as "severe and gnawing." She says that she has had this same pain in the past, but it was not as severe. She is very nauseated and had one episode of emesis in the ED that looked like dark coffee grounds.

On physical exam, she is diaphoretic and in severe discomfort. She prefers to lie quietly on the gurney without moving. Her blood pressure is 100/60, her pulse is 130, respirations are 22, and temperature is 37.2°C (98.9°F). Her abdomen is distended, and there are no bowel sounds appreciated. She has severe tenderness in the epigastric region to mild palpation with some involuntary guarding. She cries out in pain when you shake her bed and tap her heel. Her rectal exam reveals normal tone, no masses, and dark stool that is guaiac positive. The most likely diagnosis in this patient is:

A. Acute pancreatitis

B. Perforated peptic ulcer

C. Bleeding esophageal varices

D. A ruptured appendix

E. Ischemic bowel

QUESTION 5

A 26-year-old heavily menstruating female presents with anemia. All of the following laboratory values are associated with iron deficiency anemia EXCEPT:

A. Low MCV (<80)

B. High RDW (>14)

C. High red blood cell protoporphyrin level

D. High reticulocyte count

E. Low ferritin

QUESTION 6

A 20-year-old college student has a 3-day history of worsening cough productive of foul-smelling sputum. He has had 1 day of fevers to 39°C (102°F). The patient has been previously healthy. He has recently returned from traveling around the United States, including New England and the Southwest. He has a new kitten at home. Approximately 1 week ago, he was out drinking with friends. At that time he became very intoxicated, vomited several times, and passed out. A chest x-ray shows a right upper-lobe infiltrate. What is the most likely cause of this infiltrate?

A. Toxoplasmosis

B. Pneumonia secondary to gram-negative aerobes

C. Pulmonary coccidiodomycosis

D. Pneumonia secondary to anaerobes

E. Chemical pneumonitis

QUESTION 7

A 28-year-old man is "found down" in a city park. He is found to have abnormal electrolytes and ABGs consistent with a severe anion gap acidosis. Each of the following are causes of an increased anion gap acidosis EXCEPT:

A. Diabetic ketoacidosis

B. Lactic acidosis

C. Salicylate toxicity

D. Renal failure

E. Isopropyl alcohol toxicity

QUESTION 8

A 32-year-old black female presents with a 3-month history of nonproductive cough and dyspnea, especially with climbing stairs. She reports intermittent fevers to 39°C (102°F) and a 3.5 kg weight loss. She reports some pleuritic-type chest pain with cough. She denies hemoptysis, palpitations, and nausea. On further questioning, the patient also complains of wrist and ankle pain, which has interfered with her work as a nursing assistant on the obstetrics ward. She also has red nodules over her lower legs. The patient smokes two packs per day and drinks only on the weekends. Complete blood count is normal, and a serum ANA is negative. What is the most likely diagnosis?

A. Goodpasture's disease

B. Histoplasmosis

C. Systemic lupus erythematosis

D. Sarcoidosis

E. Adenocarcinoma of the lung

QUESTION 9

A 70-year-old man with known metastatic prostate cancer is admitted for pleuritic right chest pain and mild dyspnea. He has a pulse of 110, a respiratory rate of 24, and a BP of 140/80. His oxygen saturation is 86% and he is febrile with a temperature of 38.3°C (101°F). His pulmonary exam and chest x-ray are unremarkable, and his heart exam demonstrates a loud second component of S2 over the second left intercostal space. His EKG shows sinus tachycardia and his lower extremity exam is free of edema or tenderness. There is no hemoptysis or cough. What is the most appropriate diagnostic step?

A. V/Q (Ventilation perfusion) scan

B. Cardiac catheterization

C. Induced sputum collection for gram stain and cultures

D. Echocardiogram

E. D-dimer levels

QUESTION 10

A 28-year-old woman presents with the subacute onset of anterior neck pain, lowgrade fever, heat intolerance, irritability, and nervousness. She had a flu-like syndrome a week ago. She has tachycardia and a very tender thyroid gland on exam, but no proptosis or pre-tibial skin changes. She has an elevated free T4 and a low TSH. Which of the following statements best describes the situation?

A. She has Graves' disease and should have increased uptake on a radioactive iodine uptake scan.

B. She has subacute DeQuervain's thyroiditis and should have increased uptake on a radioactive iodine uptake scan.

C. She has Hashimoto's thyroiditis and should have increased uptake on a radioactive iodine uptake scan.

D. She has subacute DeQuervain's thyroiditis and should have diminished uptake on a radioactive iodine uptake scan.

E. She has Graves' disease and should have diminished uptake on a radioactive iodine uptake scan.

QUESTION 11

A 14-year-old girl has had recurrent episodes of pneumonia and bronchitis over many years. Now she presents with a 5-month history of diarrhea. She has several episodes of loose stools per day. She states that her stools are foul-smelling and oily, but she denies any blood or "tarry" stools. She has lost 4 kg. The diarrhea temporarily improves when the patient skips meals. Her mother reports that when the patient was an infant, she had surgery for "stool that was stuck inside her intestines and got really hard, like concrete." Which test will most likely yield this patient's diagnosis?

A. Stool for O&P

B. Colonoscopy

C. Sweat chloride

D. Complement levels

E. Serum test for *Helicobacter pylori*

QUESTION 12

A 23-year-old man comes to your office with a complaint of rectal pain. He has had several episodes a day of loose stools containing bright red blood for the past 3 weeks. He had a similar episode 6 months ago that resolved over a couple of weeks. On review of systems, he has a skin lesion on his right lower leg that started as a pustule and has ulcerated and enlarged over the past 2 weeks. He has had some subjective fevers and malaise. He denies recent travel or homosexual activity.

Physical exam reveals an ill-appearing man with blood pressure of 108/65, pulse is 102, respirations are 16, and temperature is 99.2. Skin exam reveals a 1-cm moderately deep necrotic ulcer with a violaceous, edematous border on the right calf. His abdomen has normal bowel sounds and is nondistended. He has some tenderness in the left lower quadrant with voluntary guarding. Rectal exam reveals an anal fissure with surrounding erythema and exquisite tenderness. A flexible sigmoidoscopy is performed and reveals diffuse inflammation of the anus, rectum, and the signoid colon. Rectal biopsy reveals crypt abscesses and pseudopolyps. Which of the following statements is TRUE about his disease?

A. After 10 years of active disease, this patient would be extremely high risk for developing colon cancer.

B. Antibiotics are used routinely in the treatment of his disease with good results.

C. Complications of his disease include bowel obstruction and fistula formation.

D. The skin lesion seen on this patient is erythema nodosum.

E. This bowel disease occurs more often in black populations than in white.

QUESTION 13

A 55-year-old man is found to be anemic on routine blood tests. His lab values are as follows:

WBC 6.0 (4.5–1 1)

Hemoglobin 10.2 (13.5–17.5)

Hematocrit 31.0 (41.0–53.0)

Platelets 225 (150–400)

MCV 110 (80–100)

RDW 15.0 (11.5–14.5)

Corrected reticulocyte count = 1%

Which of the following is the LEAST likely explanation of his anemia?

A. He is an alcohol abuser.

B. He is on methotrexate.

C. He has hypothyroidism.

D. He has autoimmune hemolytic anemia.

E. He has dysplastic anemia.

QUESTION 14

Which of the following is *not* associated with hilar adenopathy on chest x-ray?

A. Tuberculosis

B. Lymphoma

C. *Pneumocystis carinii* pneumonia

D. Histoplasmosis

E. Sarcoidosis

QUESTION 15

A 60-year-old man comes to the emergency department with confusion and altered mental status. In the ER, he has a generalized tonic clonic seizure. His wife tells you that he was placed on a thiazide diuretic for hypertension by his primary care doctor 1 week ago. Which of the following electrolyte disturbances is he most likely to have that could explain his mental status and seizure?

A. Hyponatremia

B. Hypernatremia

C. Hyperkalemia

D. Hypokalemia

E. None of the above

QUESTION 16

A 19-year-old female college student presents to the Student Health Center complaining of right knee pain and swelling for 1 day. She reports significant pain in several joints, including both wrists, her left shoulder, her right ankle, and both hips. She says that her left knee was swollen and painful nearly a week ago but is fine now. She has been previously healthy. She has not experienced any trauma. She drinks alcohol on the weekends, but denies smoking or using IV drugs. She has had three sexual partners within the past year. She was camping in Connecticut 2 weeks ago. On exam, the right knee is swollen with an effusion. The knee has decreased range of motion secondary to pain. The patient's temperature is 38.0°C (100.3°F). The patient also has a rash consisting of small pustules with necrotic centers on her hands and forearms. What is the most likely diagnosis?

A. Rheumatoid arthritis

B. Pseudogout

C. Gonococcal arthritis

D. Fibromyalgia

E. Lyme disease

QUESTION 17

What is the most common cause of death in people over the age of 45 in the United States?

A. Cancer

B. Motor vehicle accidents

C. Stroke

D. AIDS

E. Coronary artery disease

QUESTION 18

A 45-year-old woman with a history of anxious depression and obesity presents with palpitations and an increase in anxiety. She has had problems concentrating on her job as a nurse aid and has noted some heat intolerance. Her daughter has Graves' disease, which was treated with radioablation, and now takes thyroid replacement. The patient has resting tachycardia, warm moist skin, and tremor. Her thyroid gland is small and nontender. There are no manifestations of Graves' disease on exam. Her TSH is low and her free T_4 level is high. Her antithyroglobulin antibodies and antimicrosomal (antiperoxidase) antibodies are normal. She has low iodine uptake on thyroid scan. What is the most likely diagnosis?

A. Toxic multinodular goiter

B. TSH secreting pituitary tumor

C. Graves' disease

D. Subacute thyroiditis

E. Exogenous thyroid hormone ingestion

QUESTION 19

A 49-year-old white male presents with the complaint of frequently falling asleep at work. He works as an accountant and states that he often finds himself "nodding off" at his desk. Upon further questioning, the patient states that he goes to sleep and awakens at the same time each day, and does not awaken at night. His wife does not sleep in the same room with him due to the fact that his loud snoring keeps her awake. The patient drinks 1–2 cups of coffee per day and denies alcohol, tobacco, and other medications. He denies hallucinations or vivid dreams. He also denies "drop attacks." When questioned about family history, the patient only states that his elderly mother has difficulty sleeping at night because "her legs move around and wake her up."

Examination reveals a pleasant and cooperative man. He is afebrile with a pulse of 88 and blood pressure of 136/86. Pulse oximetry is 92% on room air. Height is 175 cm and weight is 127 kg. HEENT exam shows nasal septum to be midline and throat without exudate and a somewhat "crowded" oropharynx. Lungs are clear to auscultation. Heart is regular rate and rhythm with occasional ectopic beats but no murmurs. Abdomen is normal. There is no pedal edema, and pulses are brisk in all extremities. Neuro exam is nonfocal.

What is the most likely diagnosis?

A. Narcolepsy

B. Obstructive sleep apnea

C. Primary snoring

D. Restless leg syndrome

E. Poor sleep hygiene

QUESTION 20

There are many physical exam findings that are seen in patients with chronic liver disease. Which of the following physical findings is NOT seen in chronic liver disease?

A. Telangiectasias (spider angiomas)

B. Internal hemorrhoids

C. Splenomegaly

D. Testicular enlargement

E. Palmar erythema

QUESTION 21

All of the following laboratory tests are consistent with a hemolytic anemia EXCEPT:

A. Elevated corrected reticulocyte count

B. Elevated LDH

C. Spherocytes seen on the peripheral smear

D. Elevated indirect bilirubin

E. Elevated haptoglobin

QUESTION 22

A 19-year-old female college student comes to her primary care physician's office complaining of a sore throat. She had been previously healthy. She wants to know if she needs antibiotics for her throat infection.

Which of the following is not associated with streptococcal pharyngitis?

A. Tender anterior cervical lymph nodes

B. Cough

C. Fever

D. Headache

E. Pharyngeal and tonsillar exudates

QUESTION 23

A 35-year-old man comes to the ER with complaints of severe left flank pain that started approximately 2 hr ago. The pain radiates to the left groin and is sharp and 9/10 in severity. He has had one episode of nausea and vomiting with the pain. He denies fever.

On physical exam, he is extremely uncomfortable and writhing on the bed. His blood pressure is 150/100, and his pulse is 100. His temperature and respiratory rate are normal. His exam is normal except for some mild left costovertebral angle tenderness. His CBC, electrolytes, and renal function are all normal. His urinalysis showed 1+ blood, and urine culture is negative. An intravenous pyelogram (IVP) showed a round radiodense opacity in the proximal left ureter with minimal left hydronephrosis. What is his kidney stone most likely to be composed of?

A. Uric acid

B. Struvite

C. Cystine

D. Calcium oxalate

E. None of the above

QUESTION 24

A 55-year-old male presents to an Urgent Care Center complaining of severe knee pain which has been worsening over the past 2 days. He denies any trauma to the area. When questioned about his medical history, the patient reports that he is being treated with coumadin for an artificial mitral valve following rheumatic fever as a child. He also takes medication for hypothyroidism. On examination, the patient has a temperature of 38°C (100.3°F). His left knee is warm, erythematous, and tender. There is a large effusion in the knee joint. He has painful limitation of motion of the knee. He has no rashes, and no other joints are involved. Arthrocentesis is performed and shows 75,000 WBC/mm^3. A polarizing microscope shows rhomboid, positively birefringent crystals in the fluid. What is this patient's diagnosis?

A. Gout

B. Pseudogout

C. Septic arthritis

D. Rheumatoid arthritis

E. Hemarthrosis

QUESTION 25

A 62-year-old man with a history of diabetes, tobacco use, and hyperlipidemia presents with 1 hr of continuous chest pressure and 3 mm of ST-segment elevation in the anteroseptal leads of the EKG. What is the most likely pathophysiologic mechanism of this picture?

A. A coronary vessel with an underlying 95% occlusive atherosclerotic lesion

B. A coronary vessel with a 50% stenosis and superimposed coronary spasm

C. Inflammation of the pericardial lining

D. A coronary vessel with an underlying 45% occlusive atherosclerotic lesion with a superimposed plaque rupture and acute thrombus formation

E. A tear of a thoracic aortic aneurysm

QUESTION 26

A 45-year-old woman presents with symptoms and physical signs suspicious of hyperthyroidism. You obtain a TSH test and it is very low, seemingly confirming your suspicion, but the serum-free T$_4$ test is within normal limits. What test should you order now?

A. Cosyntropin stimulation test

B. Serum T$_3$

C. CT scan of the sella

D. Thyroid binding globulin

E. None of the above

QUESTION 27

A 17-year-old white female has just moved into the area and is seeking a new primary care provider. She has a history of asthma, for which she has been hospitalized twice in the past. She has never required intubation. She states that she usually needs a burst of steroids for worsening symptoms 3–4 times per year, mainly in the spring and fall. She currently uses an albuterol metered-dose inhaler 2–3 times per day. She also has a nebulizer machine and uses nebulized albuterol and atrovent for acute attacks. Examination reveals a cooperative young woman in no acute distress. Her lungs are clear to auscultation, and her expiratory phase is not prolonged. What is the best change to make to her medical management at this time?

A. Instruct the patient to use her nebulized albuterol instead of her MDI.

B. Give the patient a 5-day course of prednisone.

C. Add theophylline to the patient's daily medical regimen.

D. Tell the patient to use her metered-dose inhaler four times per day.

E. Add inhaled beclomethasone to the daily medical regimen.

QUESTION 28

A 40-year-old woman comes to the emergency department complaining of abdominal pain that started abruptly the day before. She says that her pain is constant, aching, and radiates to her back. Her abdominal pain worsened significantly when she tried to eat dinner last night. She denies fever or chills. The patient has had prior episodes of severe, colicky right upper quadrant pain and right shoulder pain in the past, and these episodes occurred after she had gone out to eat with her family. She says that this pain is different. Her only other past medical history is type 2 diabetes. She takes Metformin for her diabetes, but is not very compliant and doesn't check her sugars regularly. She smokes half-a-pack of cigarettes a day and goes out occasionally to drink margaritas with her friends.

Physical exam reveals a moderately obese woman in some distress secondary to her discomfort. She is sitting up and leaning forward and when you ask her to lie back to examine her abdomen, she says that the pain becomes worse. Her blood pressure is 140/90, pulse is 92, respirations are 18, and temperature is 100.0. Her sclera appear nonicteric, she has minimal bowel sounds, and is extremely tender to palpation in the epigastric area with voluntary guarding. She has no rebound tenderness and is not bothered when you shake the bed. Her laboratories are significant for an amylase of 200 and lipase of 1200. Her hepatic function tests are pending. Each of the following could be the cause of her pancreatitis EXCEPT:

A. Ethanol ingestion

B. Gallstone pancreatitis

C. Hypertriglyceridemia

D. Metformin

E. Pancreas divisum

QUESTION 29

A 60-year-old woman comes to your office with complaints of feeling "worn out" for the past 2 months. She has noted a 10 lb weight loss that is unintentional and some night sweats.

Physical exam reveals a pleasant, thin woman in no acute distress. Her vital signs are stable, and she is afebrile. She has slightly pale conjunctiva and mucous membranes, and she has large non-tender lymphadenopathy of her anterior cervical chain, axillae, and inguinal regions bilaterally. Her heart and lung exams are normal. Her abdomen is obese, and you think that you may feel the edge of her spleen.

Her laboratories reveal a WBC of 70,000 with 75% mature appearing lymphocytes. Her hemoglobin is 10.9 and hematocrit is 31.0. Her platelets are 120,000. Her peripheral smear shows "smudge cells," and the immunophenotyping shows the presence of CD5 with abnormally low amounts of surface immunoglobulin.

Which of the following is the most likely diagnosis?

A. Chronic lymphocytic leukemia (CLL)

B. Chronic myelogenous leukemia (CML)

C. Acute lymphocytic leukemia (ALL)

D. Acute myelogenous leukemia (AML)

E. Hairy cell leukemia

QUESTION 30

A 37-year-old male presents with a 2–3 week history of a nonproductive cough and dyspnea with exertion. He reports subjective fevers but no chills. He denies hemoptysis. He has been previously healthy, but reports a 5 kg weight loss over the past 4 months. He smokes one pack of cigarettes per day and uses IV heroin, but he denies alcohol abuse. Examination is significant for a temperature of 100.7°F, respiratory rate of 24 and pulse oximetry of 86% on room air. He has oral thrush. Lung exam reveals scattered crackles bilaterally. There is no jugular venous distension, and heart exam is normal with no murmur or gallop. Chest x-ray is shown. Sputum gram stain shows many white blood cells but no organisms. The patient had a negative PPD skin test 8 months ago. He has never been tested for HIV. What is the most likely cause of his lung findings?

A. Pulmonary tuberculosis

B. Congestive heart failure

C. *Pneumocystis carinii*

D. *Streptococcus pneumoniae*

E. *Klebsiella pneumoniae*

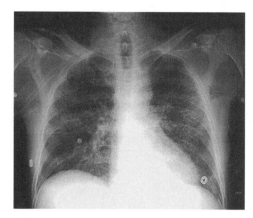

FIGURE 30

QUESTION 31

A 25-year-old woman has a father with end stage renal disease. Her paternal uncle also has renal disease, but does not yet require dialysis. The patient has the following CT scan of her abdomen (see accompanying figure) because of some hematuria and abdominal/flank pain bilaterally. Which of the following statements concerning her disease is FALSE?

A. She has a higher incidence of nephrolithiasis than a person with normal kidneys.

B. She has a higher incidence of intracranial aneurysm than a person with normal kidneys.

C. She is more likely to have mitral valve prolapse than a person with normal kidneys.

D. She is more likely to have extrarenal cysts including hepatic cysts, ovarian cysts and rarely pancreatic, splenic, and/or arachnoid cysts.

E. All of the above statements are true.

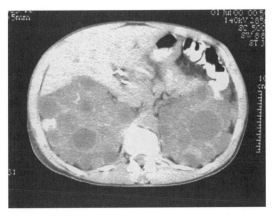

FIGURE 31

QUESTION 32

A 45-year-old woman with rheumatoid arthritis presents to the emergency department complaining of right leg pain. She states that she was in her usual state of health yesterday, but that she noticed that her right leg was swollen and painful when she got out of bed this morning. She denies any fevers, rashes, or difficulty breathing. She also denies any recent trips involving long periods of immobility. Her medications include methotrexate, naprosyn, and hydroxychloroquine. On examination, her right leg is considerably larger than the left, and she experiences pain when her foot is passively dorsiflexed. What is the next best step in management of this patient?

A. Begin a heparin drip.

B. Obtain a ventilation–perfusion scan to rule out pulmonary embolus.

C. Stop the patient's methotrexate.

D. Obtain an ultrasound with doppler of the patient's right leg.

E. Order venography of the patient's right leg.

QUESTION 33

A 42-year-old woman presents with dyspnea on exertion and more recently bouts of orthopnea and paroxysmal nocturnal dyspnea. On physical exam her lungs are clear. She has a regular rhythm on exam, with a loud first heart sound. There is also a low-pitched apical diastolic rumbling murmur that gets louder just before S1. There is a right ventricular lift. Chest radiography shows straightening of the left heart border and dilated upper lobe pulmonary veins. Which of the following is the most likely source of her symptoms?

A. Dilated cardiomyopathy

B. Aortic stenosis

C. Hypertrophic obstructive cardiomyopathy

D. Mitral stenosis

E. Aortic regurgitation

QUESTION 34

Which of the following profiles would be seen in a patient with central hypothyroidism, caused by a nonfunctioning pituitary tumor?

A. Goiter, elevated serum TSH, low serum free T_4, antimicrosomal antibodies present

B. No goiter, elevated serum TSH low serum free T_4, antimicrosomal antibodies absent

C. Goiter, low serum TSH, low serum free T_4, antimicrosomal antibodies present

D. No goiter, low serum TSH low serum free T_4, antimicrosomal antibodies absent

E. No goiter, low serum TSH normal serum free T_4, low T_3, antimicrosomal antibodies absent

QUESTION 35

A 64-year-old white female has a chest x-ray done which reveals a 1.5-cm nodule in the left upper lobe. Which of the following features would be *least* suspicious for malignancy?

A. She smoked one pack per day for 20 years but quit smoking 8 years ago

B. A clear chest x-ray 2 years ago

C. Calcifications in a "popcorn" pattern

D. A history of a positive PPD test 25 years ago that was never treated

E. The absence of hilar adenopathy

QUESTION 36

All of the following are causes of ascites with a serum-ascites albumin gradient greater than 1.1 EXCEPT:

A. Liver cirrhosis

B. Congestive heart failure

C. Budd–Chiari syndrome

D. Portal vein thrombosis

E. Peritoneal carcinomatosis

QUESTION 37

A 60-year-old man with a history of alcohol abuse and liver cirrhosis comes to the emergency department with hemoptysis. He is mildly orthostatic on exam and has a resting tachycardia. He has two large bore IVs placed, is volume resuscitated with normal saline, is typed and crossed for blood, and has his laboratories sent including a coagulation profile. Meanwhile, he is placed on IV famotidine and octreotide (for stress ulcer prophylaxis as well as treatment for the possibility of portal hypertension and variceal bleeding in a known cirrhotic patient).

On a repeat physical exam it is noted that he does not have scleral icterus. His mouth is moist with an erythematous, glossy tongue. His cardiovascular exam and lung exam are normal. He has an obese abdomen with prominent veins seen in his abdominal wall. His liver is not tender and percusses to normal size. His spleen tip is palpated easily. Rectal exam reveals internal hemorrhoids which are not bleeding. His skin reveals spider telangiectasias on his chest and mild gynecomastia.

He is found to be thrombocytopenic by laboratories with a platelet count of 85,000.

Which of the following are possible etiologies of his thrombocytopenia?

A. Alcohol toxicity

B. Platelet sequestration in the spleen

C. Famotidine

D. A and C only

E. All of the above

QUESTION 38

A 22-year-old college student has been brought to the emergency department by her roommate. She is disoriented and crying with pain from a "terrible headache." Her roommate says that she was fine yesterday but woke this morning with a headache that has gotten progressively worse over the course of the day. She has been previously healthy. She denies smoking but reports heavy alcohol use "on the weekends." She says that she has had five sexual partners in the past 2 months. Examination reveals a temperature of 103.5°F. She has no papilledema, but her neck is stiff, and she cries in pain on attempted passive neck flexion. Neuro exam is nonfocal. Skin exam reveals some purpuric lesions on her legs and feet. What is the most likely cause of this patient's confusion?

A. HSV encephalitis

B. Listeria meningitis

C. Alcohol intoxication

D. Infection with *Neisseria meningiditis*

E. Tertiary syphilis

QUESTION 39

A 60-year-old woman with a history of type 2 diabetes mellitus for the past 20 years comes to your office with a complaint of "swelling all over." She started to have pretibial edema 3 months ago, and this has progressed to diffuse leg swelling to her waist. She has gained 15–20 lb in the last 2 months and has had some shortness of breath with exertion. She denies chest pain, orthopnea, or paroxysmal nocturnal dyspnea. She has never been very compliant with her diabetes care and does not visit the doctor regularly.

On physical exam, her blood pressure is 150/90, heart rate is 84, respiratory rate is 20, and she is afebrile. She is obese, comfortable and alert, and oriented. Her neck does not have appreciable elevated jugular pressures. Her heart is regular with no murmurs, rubs, or gallops. She has slightly decreased breath sounds in her lung bases bilaterally, with dullness to percussion. Her abdomen is benign, but she has sacral edema and 3+ pitting edema to her waist.

Her labs reveal an albumin of 2.5. She has normal liver enzymes. Her coagulation panel is normal. Her urinalysis reveals 4+ protein. You think that she has nephrotic syndrome. Which of the following statements is TRUE regarding nephrotic syndrome?

A. Nephrotic range proteinuria is defined as greater than 1 g of protein per 24 hr.

B. Patients with severe proteinuria are at risk of bleeding because of the loss of protein C and S.

C. Patients with severe proteinuria are at risk of infection because of the loss of immunoglobulins.

D. Patients with nephrotic syndrome have low cholesterol levels, because of the loss of cholesterol in the oval fat bodies in the urine.

E. None of the above statements are true.

QUESTION 40

A 38-year-old white female presents with complaints of morning stiffness and joint pain in multiple joints. Which of the following does not support the diagnosis of rheumatoid arthritis?

A. Ibuprofen helps to control her pain.

B. The patient has firm nodules palpated on the extensor surfaces of her elbows.

C. The patient has involvement of her MCP and DIP joints bilaterally.

D. Periarticular erosions are seen on x-ray of her wrists.

E. The patient is found to have splenomegaly and leukopenia.

QUESTION 41

A 40-year-old executive on his first visit to your office is noted to have a systolic murmur over the upper right parastemal area with radiation over the carotids. You note a delayed and sustained pulse, a diminished A2, and an S4. Chest palpation reveals a lateralized sustained ventricular impulse. The murmur is diminished with hand grip and Valsalva maneuvers. Blood pressures are normal and equal in all extremities. He has no symptoms of angina, dyspnea, or syncope. What is the most likely etiology of his findings?

A. Hypertrophic obstructive cardiomyopathy

B. Valvular aortic stenosis secondary to a congenital bicuspid valve

C. Valvular aortic stenosis secondary to degeneration and calcification of a tricuspid valve

D. Mitral regurgitation secondary to rheumatic heart disease

E. Mitral stenosis secondary to rheumatic heart disease

QUESTION 42

Which of the following statements regarding Hashimoto's thyroiditis is TRUE?

A. Antimicrosomal (antiperoxidase) antibodies are generally present in high titers.

B. It is the most common source of hyperthyroidism associated with goiter.

C. Thyroid scans show avid iodine uptake on thyroid scanning.

D. The goiter of Hashimoto's thyroiditis is always smooth; therefore Hashimoto's is not in the differential diagnosis of a multinodular goiter.

E. Hashimoto's is most common in the adolescent age group.

QUESTION 43

A 30-year-old asthmatic is in the intensive care unit with a severe asthma exacerbation. He has been stable on the ventilator for the past 12 hours. The nurse notes that his oxygenation has suddenly dropped. On examination, the patient has diffuse expiratory wheezes on the left and absent breath sounds on the right. The patient's trachea is deviated to the left. The patient appears agitated, and his oxygen saturations have dropped to 84%. What is the most likely cause of this patient's decompensation?

A. The patient has developed a nosocomial pneumonia.

B. The patient's asthma exacerbation has worsened.

C. The patient has a mucous plug occluding the endotracheal tube.

D. The patient has severe atelectasis on the right because of lying flat in bed for so long.

E. The patient has a pneumothorax on the right.

QUESTION 44

All of the following are risk factors associated with the development of colorectal cancer EXCEPT:

A. A history of adenomatous polyps

B. Inflammatory bowel disease (ulcerative colitis and Crohn's disease)

C. The consumption of saccharine sweeteners

D. Tobacco smoking

E. Familial polyposis syndrome

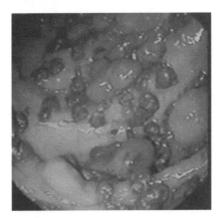

FIGURE 44

QUESTION 45

A 65-year-old man with a history of stage III squamous cell lung cancer is status post resection of the tumor and ipsilateral mediastinal lymph nodes with postoperative mediastinal radiation. He presents to the hospital 6 months later with a history of nausea and vomiting for the past few days and is now confused, dehydrated, and lethargic. Which of the following paraneoplastic syndromes would most likely explain his mental status changes?

A. Weakness from Lambert–Eaton syndrome

B. Ectopic erythropoietin production with polycythemia

C. Hypercalcemia from parathyroid hormone-related polypeptide (PTHRP) production

D. Hyponatremia from excess ADH production

E. Cushing's syndrome secondary to ACTH production

QUESTION 46

A 22-year-old male presents to the emergency department with acute groin pain. He reports that the pain has been present for 6 hr, and it is so severe that he is unable to walk. He denies dysuria, hematuria, or penile discharge. He has experienced no trauma. He has a fever to 38.3°C (101°F). On genitourinary exam, his left testicle is extremely tender to palpation with associated warmth and swelling. There is a fairly firm, tender mass palpated along the posterior aspect of the testis. Cremasteric reflex is intact, and there is no change in pain with elevation of the scrotum. There are no other abnormal physical findings. Urinalysis is positive for leukocyte esterase. Radionucleotide scan shows increased blood flow to the left testicle. What is the most likely diagnosis?

A. Testicular malignancy

B. Epididymitis

C. Testicular torsion

D. Urinary tract infection

E. Mumps orchitis

QUESTION 47

A 35-year-old woman with schizophrenia is admitted to the psychiatry ward for auditory hallucinations and psychosis. A few days later you are consulted for abnormal laboratories. They are as follows:

Sodium 125 (135–145)

Chloride 88 (95–105)

Potassium 4.0 (3.5–5.0)

Bicarbonate 24 (22–28)

BUN 10 (7–10)

Creatinine 0.9 (0.6–1.2)

Glucose 105 (70–110)

You examine the patient, and her vital signs are stable. She appears euvolemic on exam. She is oriented to person, place, and time, but is still having some auditory hallucinations and psychotic symptoms. You appropriately order some further tests:

Serum osmolality 252 (275–295)

Urine specific gravity 1.001

Urine osmolality 150 (50–1400)

Which of the following is the most likely cause of the patient's hyponatremia?

A. Pseudohyponatremia

B. Diabetes insipidus

C. Psychogenic polydipsia

D. SIADH

E. None of the above

QUESTION 48

A 38-year-old obese male with no past medical problems presents to his primary care physician with the complaint of low back pain. He states that this pain has been present for 2 weeks. He denies any history of trauma, fevers, weight loss, and bowel or bladder dysfunction. His pain is worse with walking and at the end of the day. It does not change with changes in position, and he has not noticed any change in his gait. On examination, pain is unchanged with straight leg raise. He has no focal tenderness to palpation, and sensation is completely intact. Deep tendon reflexes are 2+ at knees and ankles bilaterally, and strength is 5/5 throughout. Pedal pulses are brisk and symmetric. Which of the following is appropriate management of this patient's back pain?

A. PA and lateral x-rays of the lumbar spine

B. Conservative management with back exercises and NSAIDs

C. Bed rest for 7–10 days

D. Oral demerol as needed for pain

E. MRI of the lumbar spine

QUESTION 49

Which of the following statements regarding atrial fibrillation is true?

A. Atrial fibrillation prevalence peaks in the sixth decade of life.

B. Warfarin and aspirin are equally effective options for reducing the thromboembolic complications associated with atrial fibrillation; both reduce the risk by about 50% over control patients.

C. Patients with lone atrial fibrillation do not need to be treated with chronic warfarin anticoagulation.

D. A patient on anticoagulation prior to cardioversion should have warfarin discontinued the day after because their risk for thromboembolism has been removed once they are in sinus rhythm.

E. A patient with atrial fibrillation with a ventricular response of 150 beats per minute and symptomatic hypotension should be treated with a loading bolus of procainamide immediately.

QUESTION 50

A 30-year-old patient presents for a routine employment history and physical. You note a dominant thyroid nodule on the physical exam. All of the following findings would increase your suspicion of malignancy in the nodule EXCEPT:

A. Male sex of the patient

B. Rapid growth of the nodule

C. A history of irradiation of the tonsils as a child

D. The appearance of a "cold" nodule on thyroid scan

E. A suppressed TSH level

BLOCK TWO

QUESTIONS

QUESTION 51

A 24-year-old medical student has a routine PPD placed to test for tuberculosis. When he returns 48 hr later, there is 16 mm of induration. He had a negative test one year ago. He denies cough, fevers, night sweats, or weight loss. A chest x-ray is shown. Which of the following is the proper recommendation?

A. Isoniazid and rifampin for 3 months.

B. Send sputum for culture.

C. Begin therapy with four drugs until sputum culture results are available, then narrow coverage.

D. Repeat the PPD test in 2 weeks.

E. Isoniazid for 6 months.

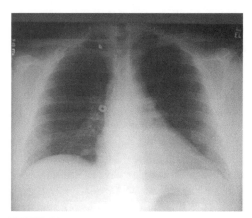

FIGURE 51

QUESTION 52

A 48-year-old woman comes to your office complaining of fatigue and pruritis. She says that she has felt itchy and tired for the past 6 months. Initially, she thought that her skin was dry, and she went to see a dermatologist for the itchiness. She has tried many lotions and soaps without relief. She denies rashes, fever, or chills. Her past medical history is significant for Raynaud's phenomenon, but she has never had any symptoms of arthritis.

Physical examination reveals a well-nourished woman in no distress. Her blood pressure is 125/75, pulse is 80, respirations are 14, and temperature is 37°C (98.7°F). She has no scleral icterus or pallor. Her neck is supple without thyromegaly or lymphadenopathy. Her heart sounds are regular without murmur, rub, or gallop. Her lungs are clear to auscultation. Her abdomen is soft and nontender without hepatosplenomegaly. Her skin is not dry and is without rashes. Her laboratories reveal an elevated alkaline phosphatase, but the rest of her liver enzymes are normal. Which of the following lab tests is appropriate to order to help you make the correct diagnosis?

A. Anti-mitochondrial antibody (AMA)

B. TSH

C. Sedimentation rate

D. alpha-I antitrypsin level

E. ceruloplasmin level

QUESTION 53

All of the following are associated with the complication of tumor lysis syndrome EXCEPT:

A. Hyperkalemia

B. Hyperphosphatemia

C. Hypercalcemia

D. Hyperuricemia

E. All of the above are associated with tumor lysis syndrome

QUESTION 54

A 65-year-old male presents complaining of severe burning pain of the skin of his left forearm. He reports that the pain started 3 days prior and has progressively worsened. It is localized to a limited area on the dorsal surface of the arm and does not radiate. He has never had anything like this before. His hand is neurovascularly intact with good radial pulse. Pain is worse with palpation of the involved area. The vesicular rash shown is present exactly in the area where he has pain. What is the most likely cause of this patient's pain?

A. Herpes simplex

B. Eczema

C. Cellulitis

D. Varicella zoster

E. Tinea corpora

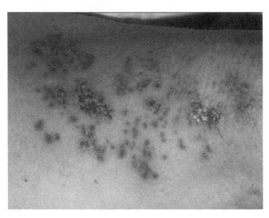

FIGURE 54

QUESTION 55

A patient is admitted to the ICU with acute renal failure. You obtain a fractional excretion of sodium and find that it is less than 1%.

A fractional excretion of sodium (FENA) of less than 1% would be expected in all of the following causes of acute renal failure EXCEPT:

A. Cardiogenic shock

B. Severe volume depletion

C. Radiocontrast nephropathy

D. Acute tubular necrosis (ATN)

E. All of the above would have a FENA <1%

QUESTION 56

A 28-year-old Japanese-American woman is referred by her gynecologist for work-up of hypertension. She has been previously healthy except for some generalized fatigue over the past 6 weeks. She has never been pregnant, and her menstrual periods are regular and without excessive bleeding. On physical exam, the patient is thin and in no acute distress. Her heart rate is 90 with a blood pressure of 150/92. On cardiac exam, she has a diastolic murmur heard best at the left lower sternal border. Radial pulses are very weak bilaterally. There are no rashes or edema. Urinalysis is normal. What is the most likely diagnosis?

A. Takayasu's arteritis

B. Membranoproliferative glomerulonephritis

C. Essential hypertension

D. Spontaneous bacterial endocarditis

E. Buerger's disease

QUESTION 57

Your 55-year-old patient suffers an anteroseptal myocardial infarction. His post infarction hospital course is uncomplicated clinically. He has frequent ventricular premature contractions on telemetry. His ejection fraction after the infarction is estimated at 38% (moderately impaired). Which statement regarding this patient is correct?

A. IV Lidocaine should be started in the hospital and then he should be transitioned to an oral antiarrhythmic.

B. Both angiotension converting enzyme inhibitors and beta-blockers improve survival in these patients.

C. Both nitrates and calcium channel blockers improve survival in these patients.

D. Coronary angiography should routinely be done in all patients prior to discharge to treat any residual coronary disease.

E. Aspirin is commonly used but has not been shown to reduce recurrent infarction or late mortality.

QUESTION 58

A 35-year-old woman presents to your office with generalized fatigue, cold intolerance, and amenorrhea since the birth of her last child 8 months ago. Her last delivery was a difficult one, and she states she had bleeding complications requiring multiple transfusions. She was unsuccessful at breast feeding her baby. She also complains of diffuse vague aches and pains, and pallor of the skin. On exam she is a pale appearing female of normal height and weight. She has no goiter. Chest and abdominal exam are normal. You note atrophic vaginitis on the pelvic exam. A serum pregnancy test is negative. You suspect hypopituitarism. Which of the following labs would support this diagnosis?

A. A high TSH and low T_4 level

B. A low serum estradiol with elevated LH and FSH

C. High levels of somatomedin-C (insulin-like growth factor)

D. A low cortisol state as defined by a low-dose cosyntropin stimulation test and an inappropriately high ACTH level

E. None of the above

QUESTION 59

A 26-year-old male who is a recent immigrant from Haiti presents with 2 months of a progressively worsening cough. He reports 3–4 episodes of hemoptysis a week for the past month and intermittent fevers and chills. He has also experienced a weight loss of 3–4 kg over 2 months. A chest x-ray reveals a left upper lobe infiltrate and perihilar lymphadenopathy. A PPD test has 11 mm of induration at 48 hr. Sputum is positive for acid fast bacilli and has been sent for culture. What is the best next step in caring for this patient?

- **A.** Begin therapy with isoniazid, rifampin, pyrazinamide, and ethambutol.
- **B.** Treat with 6 months of isoniazid only.
- **C.** Wait for the culture results before beginning therapy.
- **D.** Treat with isoniazid, rifampin, and pyrazinamide for 6 months.
- **E.** There is no need to treat because the PPD is negative.

QUESTION 60

A 50-year-old man comes to your office with the complaint of abdominal pain, nausea, and chest "burning" which has occurred intermittently for the past five years. He says the discomfort occurs throughout the day and he often wakes up at night with a bad taste in his mouth and chest "burning." He feels bloated and "belchy" during these episodes of discomfort. He has taken over the counter antacid medications with minimal relief. He denies dysphagia, odynophagia, or hematemesis. His bowel movements are regular and he denies melena or rectal bleeding. He smokes a pack of cigarettes a day and has done so for 30 years. He drinks a beer or two each evening when he gets home from work. He works as a business executive and often takes clients to late evening dinner meetings.

On physical exam, he is moderately obese, comfortable, and in no distress. Blood pressure is 145/90, pulse is 80, respirations are 18, and temperature is 36.6°C (97.8°F). His physical exam, other than obesity, is normal. Which of the following is NOT a complication of his disease?

- **A.** Peptic stricture
- **B.** Schatzki's ring
- **C.** Barrett's esophagus
- **D.** Erosive esophagitis
- **E.** Adenocarcinoma of the esophagus

QUESTION 61

All of the following statements are true about breast cancer EXCEPT:

A. Twelve percent of women will develop breast cancer in their lifetime, and 3.5% of women will die of breast cancer.

B. The median age of women with breast cancer is 54 years old, and the risk increases with age.

C. Patients with a first degree relative with breast cancer have a relative risk of 1.5–2 times that of patients without a first degree relative with breast cancer. The risk is even higher if the relative had premenopausal breast cancer or bilateral breast cancer.

D. A long duration of estrogen exposure, such as in women with early menarche and/or late menopause, appears to predispose them to an increased risk of breast cancer.

E. Seventy to eighty percent of women with breast cancer have an identifiable risk factor.

QUESTION 62

A 17-year-old female comes to an Urgent Care Center for abdominal pain and fever. She reports a 2-day history of worsening abdominal pain accompanied by nausea and fevers. She has had no emesis or change in bowel habits. She denies dysuria, hematuria, or blood in her stools. Her last menstrual period ended 1 week ago and was normal. She uses tampons. She denies tobacco and alcohol use. She has had unprotected sexual intercourse with two different partners within the past 3 months. Physical exam reveals a temperature of 38.9°C (102°F). Abdominal exam is significant only for suprapubic tenderness. Pelvic exam reveals a thin mucopurulent cervical discharge and cervical motion tenderness, but no adnexal or uterine masses are appreciated. What is the most likely diagnosis?

A. Urinary tract infection

B. Pelvic inflammatory disease

C. Toxic shock syndrome

D. Bacterial vaginosis

E. Cervical trichomonas

QUESTION 63

All of the following statements regarding hematuria are true EXCEPT:

A. A urine dipstick is not specific for blood. False positives include myoglobin and free hemoglobin.

B. Neoplasms of the urinary tract account for 15–20% of patients with hematuria after age 40, but two-thirds of these are benign polyps.

C. Urinary tract calculi are a common cause of hematuria in adults.

D. Urinary tract infection is a frequent cause of hematuria in children and adults.

E. Deformed red cells or red cell casts seen on microscopic analysis suggests a glomerular source of bleeding.

QUESTION 64

A 41-year-old female presents for evaluation of recurrent sinusitis. She states that she has been treated for sinusitis several times a year over the past three years. She has also had generalized fatigue and a 4 kg weight loss over the past 9 months. Physical examination of the chest reveals scattered crackles bilaterally. A chest x-ray shows multiple bilateral cavitary lesions consistent with granulomas, but no hilar adenopathy. Urinalysis shows 2+ blood and 2+ protein. Microscopic examination of the urine shows red cell casts. Laboratory studies show a mildly elevated sedimentation rate, negative ANA, and a positive antineutrophil cytoplasmic antibody. What is the most likely diagnosis?

A. Goodpasture's syndrome

B. Polyarteritis nodosa

C. Systemic lupus erythematosis

D. Wegener's granulomatosis

E. Sarcoidosis

QUESTION 65

A 60-year-old woman with a long history of diabetes and hypertension presents with increasing dyspnea, orthopnea, and pedal edema. She denies angina or recent change in diet. An EKG shows sinus tachycardia at a rate of 110 beats per minute, and she is tachypneic. She has bibasilar rales, mild JVD, but no murmurs or S3 on cardiac exam. Her chest x-ray is consistent with mild pulmonary edema and cardiomegaly, while an echo shows diminished LV dysfunction and an estimated EF of 35%. Which of the following medications has been shown to reduce mortality rates in this patient?

A. Digoxin

B. Furosemide

C. Nitrates

D. ACE inhibitors

E. Dobutamine

QUESTION 66

Your patient is found to have hyponatremia secondary to SIADH. Which of the following would be potentially useful in this patient?

A. Chloropropamide (Diabinese)

B. Hypotonic saline

C. Carbemazepine

D. Demeclocycline

E. Desmopressin

QUESTION 67

A 71-year-old male presents with a 1-mg standing cough. He tells you that this cough has been present for several years but has gradually worsened over the past year. He produces several tablespoons of white sputum each day, but there has been no recent change in amount or quality of sputum. He denies hemoptysis, fevers, and chills. He has dyspnea when he walks up a flight of stairs. He tells you that he has lost 2–3 kg over the past year. Past medical history is significant for a diagnosis of COPD and a 60-pack year smoking history. Medications include inhaled ipratropium bromide, albuterol, and theophylline.

On physical exam, the patient is very thin and has a barrel chest. He is in no significant distress and can speak in full sentences. His respiratory rate is 16 breaths per minute. His heart sounds are diminished. Respirations are slightly diminished in the lung bases bilaterally with a prolonged expiratory phase and minimal scattered wheezes. A few scattered crackles are also noted bilaterally. Extremities show no clubbing or edema, and there is no jugular venous distension. A blood gas is performed which shows a PaO_2 of 62 and a $PaCO_2$ of 58. A chest x-ray shows hyperinflation but no infiltrate. What is the best management for this patient now?

A. Obtain a sputum culture and start PO erythromycin.

B. Check pulmonary function tests.

C. Provide the patient with a cough suppressant containing codeine.

D. Arrange for a diagnostic bronchoscopy.

E. Arrange for home oxygen therapy.

QUESTION 68

When comparing a duodenal ulcer to a gastric ulcer, which of the following statements are FALSE?

A. *Helicobacter pylori* infection is directly correlated to more duodenal ulcers than gastric ulcers.

B. Patients with gastric ulcers have INCREASED gastric acid secretion, and patients with duodenal ulcers have NORMAL or DECREASED gastric acid secretion.

C. Patients with duodenal ulcers classically have pain 2–3 hr after a meal and their pain is relieved by food intake; whereas patients with gastric ulcers may have pain that is worsened by eating.

D. NSAIDs account for more gastric ulcers than duodenal ulcers.

E. Patients with gastric ulcers found on EGD need to have a repeat scoping procedure in 2–3 months after completion of the antimicrobial therapy for *H. pylori* and acid suppression therapy, to make sure that their ulcer has healed. Biopsies must be taken to evaluate for malignancy in a poorly healing gastric ulcer.

QUESTION 69

A 34-year-old male presents with several weeks of hemoptysis. He has had no fevers, chills, or weight loss. He denies any ill contacts. He now reports a few days of intermittent hematuria, but he denies dysuria and abdominal or back pain. Urinalysis reveals 1+ protein, 2+ blood with many RBCs and red blood cell casts seen on microscopic evaluation. Chest x-ray shows diffuse bilateral infiltrates. A renal biopsy is positive for anti-basement membrane antibodies. Which of the following is the most likely cause of this patient's hemoptysis?

A. Wegener's granulomatosis

B. Systemic lupus erythematosis

C. Factor IX deficiency (Christmas disease)

D. Post-infectious glomerulonephritis

E. Goodpasture's syndrome

QUESTION 70

A 21-year-old college student comes to the Student Health Center because he is afraid that he has had a stroke. He states that he woke up this morning unable to move the right side of his face. He denies fevers, visual changes, rashes, or trauma. However, he does report that he has had bilateral knee pain for the past 3–4 days. The patient has been previously healthy and active, although he reports that he had a bad case of "the flu" approximately 2 months ago, which included the rash pictured. He denies drug, alcohol, or tobacco abuse. He went on a hiking and camping trip 2–3 months ago in Wisconsin with his botany class. Physical exam reveals bilateral knee effusions and pain with active ROM. The patient has a right facial droop, including the muscles of the forehead on that side. He is afebrile, and the remainder of his physical exam is within normal limits. What is the most likely diagnosis?

A. Left-sided CVA

B. Erythema multiforme

C. Myasthenia gravis

D. *Borrelia burgdorferi* infection

E. Post-viral autoimmune syndrome

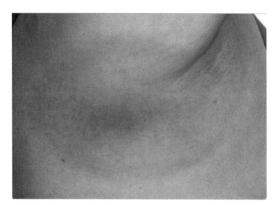

FIGURE 70

QUESTION 71

A 55-year-old woman with end stage renal disease due to lupus is on hemodialysis. She did not go to her past two hemodialysis appointments, and presents to the emergency room complaining of shortness of breath, orthopnea, and lower extremity swelling. Her physical exam reveals a blood pressure of 160/100, respiratory rate of 24, and oxygen saturation on room air of 88%, and she is afebrile. She is tachypneic and using some accessory muscles to breathe. Her jugular venous pressure is elevated, and she has inspiratory crackles half way up her posterior lung fields. Her heart is regular with an S4. There are no murmurs. She has the EKG pictured below.

Which of the following interventions should you do FIRST?

A. Give IV calcium gluconate or calcium citrate.

B. Give IV furosemide.

C. Give IV glucose and insulin.

D. Give PO or retention enema of sodium polystyrene sulfonate.

E. Give high dose albuterol nebulizer treatments.

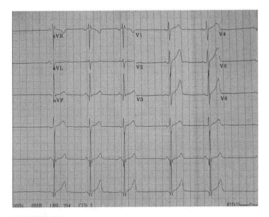

FIGURE 71

QUESTION 72

A 45-year-old white male IV drug user presents to his primary care physician's office complaining of a purplish rash on his arms and feet. He states that the rash has been present for nearly 2 weeks, and is progressively worsening. It is not pruritic or painful. He has a long history of IV drug and alcohol abuse, but no underlying medical problems.

On physical exam, he has a blood pressure of 160/94 and pulse rate of 88. He is in no acute distress, and heart and lung exam are normal. Sclera are mildly icteric. Abdominal exam is significant for mild right upper quadrant tenderness and a liver edge palpated 5 cm below the right costal margin. Skin exam reveals a palpable purpura on both arms and his left foot. His right lower extremity has both some purpura and livedo reticularis. Neurologic exam reveals both decreased strength (plantar flexion) and decreased sensation of the left foot. A urinalysis reveals microscopic hematuria and mild proteinuria without leukocytes or nitrite. An HIV test is negative. A hepatitis panel reveals that the patient has hepatitis B. What is the most likely cause of his "rash"?

A. Polyarteritis nodosa

B. Henoch–Schonlein purpura

C. Idiopathic thrombocytopenic purpura

D. Decreased coagulation factors secondary to liver cirrhosis from hepatitis B

E. Kaposi's sarcoma

QUESTION 73

Your patient has been hospitalized for pulmonary edema and is diagnosed with CHF secondary to dilated cardiomyopathy. You are counseling him about different medications used in the treatment of CHF secondary to dilated cardiomyopathy. Which medications do you tell your patient have been shown to decrease the substantial mortality rates of CHF?

A. Digoxin, furosemide, and ACE inhibitors

B. ACE inhibitors, coumadin, and digoxin

C. Aldactone, ACE inhibitors, and beta-blockers

D. Dobutamine, ACE inhibitors, and beta-blockers

E. Hydralazine, nitrates, and amlodipine

QUESTION 74

A 21-year-old young man is brought into the ER for first time seizure activity. In the field his glucose level is low at 25 and he stops seizing with infusion of concentrated dextrose. He is hypotensive with a systolic BP of 80 that corrected to 100 with IV normal saline. In the ER he remains somnolent and unable to give any history. Other lab findings include moderate hyponatremia and hyperkalemia, and a mild non-anion gap acidosis. His parents are contacted and they report personality changes, a decline in vitality and energy, and a 10 lb weight loss in the past year. You note that the patient seems to have a tan although the patient's family reports he has stopped most outdoor activities over the last year. The palms of his hands look pale but have dark hand crease lines as shown in the figure, and scars look pigmented as well. What is the most likely diagnosis?

A. Aspirin overdose

B. Cushing's disease

C. Addison's disease (primary adrenal insufficiency)

D. Adrenal failure secondary to withdrawal of surreptitious steroid use

E. Panhypopituitarism

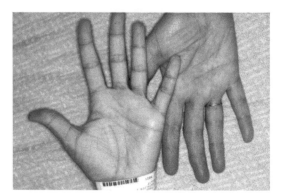

FIGURE 74

QUESTION 75

A 19-year-old white female presents with a non-productive cough. She says that the cough has been present for 3 weeks now. She has also noticed some nasal congestion and says that her eyes get "itchy" in the evenings. She denies shortness of breath, wheezing, fevers, or hemoptysis. She has had similar problems in the past, always in the spring and fall. She has no pets. She smokes half-a-pack of cigarettes per day. On physical exam, the patient is afebrile and is not in respiratory distress. She has mild bilateral conjunctival injection. Her nasal turbinates are boggy and have a bluish tinge. She has mild tenderness to percussion over the maxillary sinuses, and there is a small amount of drainage in her posterior pharynx. Lungs are clear to auscultation bilaterally and without wheezing.

What is the most likely cause of her cough?

A. Acute bronchitis

B. Smoker's cough

C. Bacterial sinusitis

D. Allergic rhinitis

E. Chronic bronchitis

QUESTION 76

A 52-year-old man with liver cirrhosis due to alcohol abuse is taken to the emergency room because he "is not acting right." The patient has been confused for the last day and this morning, he was difficult to awaken. When his wife was finally able to awaken him, he was speaking incoherently.

On physical exam, his blood pressure is 108/60, his pulse is 106, respirations are 22, and temperature is 36.6°C (97.9°F). He is awake but very confused and disoriented. His sclera are icteric and his skin is jaundiced. He has dry mucous membranes and a bright red erythematous tongue. His heart is tachycardic and regular without murmurs, rubs, or gallops. His lungs are clear to ascultation. His abdomen is distended and firm with low pitched, hypoactive bowel sounds, and it is dull to percussion. It is hard to assess if the patient's abdomen is tender because of his neurological impairment. His extremities reveal a trace of edema bilaterally, and his neurologic exam reveals asterixis. Which of the following are possible precipitants of his hepatic encephalopathy?

A. Spontaneous bacterial peritonitis (SBP)

B. Dehydration and hypokalemia

C. Gastrointestinal bleeding

D. A and C

E. All of the above

QUESTION 77

Which of the following patients does not need to be given the hepatitis B vaccine?

A. A 23-year-old female with no medical problems who uses IV heroin

B. A 1-week-old male infant whose mother had negative Hep B serology

C. A 56-year-old male with diabetes mellitus and renal failure on chronic peritoneal dialysis

D. A 58-year-old male with alcohol-induced cirrhosis and hepatitis C

E. A healthy 12-year-old female with no known medical problems

QUESTION 78

A 55-year-old man with a history of diabetes mellitus type 2 and proteinuria related to his diabetes comes to your office for a new patient visit. He has no complaints, although on physical exam he has changes consistent with retinopathy and neuropathy from his diabetes. He has no intrinsic lung disease. His serum chemistry reveals the following:

Sodium 136 (135–146)

Potassium 5.3 (3.5–5.0)

Chloride 109 (95–105)

HCO_3^- 16 (22–28)

BUN 30 (7–18)

Creatinine 2.0 (0.6–1.2)

Glucose 150 (80–110)

You ask the patient if he has had any problems with diarrhea and he denies this. What is the most likely cause of his electrolyte abnormalities?

A. He has an anion gap acidosis from DKA.

B. He has an anion gap acidosis from acute renal failure.

C. He has a non-anion gap acidosis from a distal renal tubular acidosis.

D. He has a non-anion gap acidosis from vomiting.

E. None of the above.

QUESTION 79

A 42-year-old male with rheumatoid arthritis presents with one day of left knee pain. He denies trauma to the knee. His medications include methotrexate, prednisone, and ranitidine. On physical exam, he has a temperature of 38.0°C (100.4°F). His knee is warm and tender to palpation with a large effusion. He has decreased range of motion in the joint secondary to pain. Arthrocentesis reveals 110,000 WBC/mm^3 and 8,000 RBC/mm^3. Gram stain is negative for organisms. What is the most likely cause of his knee pain?

A. Exacerbation of his rheumatoid arthritis

B. Osteoarthritis

C. Septic joint

D. Felty's syndrome

E. Hemarthrosis

QUESTION 80

A 60-year-old man with a long history of poorly controlled hypertension presents with dyspnea and acute mild pulmonary edema. EKG and echocardiogram are unremarkable except for findings consistent with LVH (left ventricular hypertrophy), and he has no history of angina. What is the most likely cause of his symptoms?

A. Diastolic dysfunction because of LVH

B. Dilated cardiomyopathy

C. Diastolic dysfunction secondary to restrictive cardiomyopathy

D. Coronary artery disease

E. Mitral stenosis

QUESTION 81

A 46-year-old man presents to your office for high blood pressure and diabetes. The patient complains of a 40 lb weight gain over the last 2 years, and the hypertension and diabetes have both been diagnosed in the last year. You note that he has centripetal obesity, striae, and a "buffalo hump" fat pad. What would be the most appropriate next step to take?

A. Check a 24-hr urinary free cortisol.

B. Order a MRI with special attention to the pituitary region.

C. Order a TSH test.

D. Send the patient to a dietician and follow up in 3 months.

E. Check an ACTH level.

QUESTION 82

A 58-year-old white male presents with a history of worsening dyspnea and cough over the past 9 months. His cough is not productive, and he denies fevers or weight loss. The patient works as a cattle farmer in Arizona. He notes that his symptoms improved while on a vacation to Florida 2 months ago. He has smoked one pack of cigarettes per day for 40 years. Lung exam is significant for scattered rales bilaterally. Cardiac exam reveals no murmurs or gallops. The patient has no edema or jugular venous distension. A chest x-ray shows bilateral infiltrates. Pulmonary function tests show a restrictive pattern with decreased diffusion capacity. What is the most likely diagnosis?

A. Community acquired pneumonia

B. Hypersensitivity pneumonitis

C. Chronic obstructive pulmonary disease

D. Coccidioidomycosis

E. Congestive heart failure

QUESTION 83

All of the following statements about sponta-neous bacterial peritonitis (SBP) are true EXCEPT:

A.   Ascitic fluid with low protein content is more susceptible to bacterial infection.

B.   Clinical symptoms of SBP such as fever and abdominal tenderness may be absent.

C.   The diagnosis is made when the ascitic fluid cell count reveals greater than 250 lympho-cytes per microliter.

D.   Enteric gram negative bacilli are the causa-tive organism in the majority of cases.

E.   The pathogenesis of SBP is thought to occur by the transmigration of enteric bacteria through the bowel wall and lymphatics into the blood stream and hematogenous infection of the ascites fluid.

QUESTION 84

A 47-year-old white female has been hospital-ized in the intensive care unit for 10 days. She was hospitalized for septic shock, and work-up revealed a pelvic abscess which was thought to be secondary to surgical complications from a recent total abdominal hysterectomy. The abscess was surgically drained, and she has improved on broad-spectrum intravenous antibi-otics, including ampicillin, gentamicin, and clin-damycin. Her blood pressure stabilized, she was extubated without complications and was trans-ferred to the floor on day 10 of her hospitaliza-tion. That day, she was noted to have new onset of non-bloody, watery diarrhea. She had no nausea or vomiting, but the diarrhea occurred 6–8 times per day, and she experienced some diffuse crampy lower abdominal pain. Stool is guaiac negative and contains no mucus. Which of the following is the best test for diagnosis of the cause of her diarrhea?

A.   Stool cultures

B.   Stool for O&P

C.   Colonoscopy

D.   Stool for C. difficile toxin

E.   Fecal fat collection

QUESTION 85

A 70-year-old man comes to the emergency room with complaints of nausea and fatigue for the past 2 days. His vital signs are within normal limits. He is found to be in acute renal failure by laboratories. Which of the following is the most appropriate next step in management of this patient?

A. Placement of a central line for hemodialysis

B. Placement of a foley catheter

C. Obtain a blood gas to determine his acid/base status

D. Renal ultrasound

E. Intravenous pyclogram

QUESTION 86

A 35-year-old female presents with sudden onset of right arm and leg weakness. Past medical history is significant for systemic lupus erythematosis and resultant renal insufficiency. She was hospitalized with a pulmonary embolus 3 years ago, and she had a deep venous thrombosis of the right leg 5 years ago. Her medications include prednisone and cyclophosphamide. Physical exam reveals a patient that is afebrile and in no acute distress. She has no nuchal rigidity. Cardiopulmonary exam is normal. Neurologic examination is significant for weakness of right arm and leg. Cranial nerves are all intact. Babinski test shows an up-going right toe. What is the most likely cause of this patient's problem?

A. Lupus cerebritis

B. Bacterial meningitis

C. Uremic encephalopathy

D. Anti-phospholipid antibody syndrome

E. Steroid psychosis

QUESTION 87

A 70-year-old man with a history of tobacco use and hypertension presents to the ER with indigestion 1 hr after eating a large meal. He had some relief with antacids, but the discomfort had recurred. In the ER he was immediately given aspirin, oxygen, and nitroglycerin with near total relief of his symptoms. His EKG shows a sinus rhythm and a left bundle branch block. The left bundle branch block was not present on an EKG obtained in the clinic 1 month ago. His blood pressure is 160/90. What would be the most appropriate next step in his treatment?

A. Discharge home with nitrates and H2 blockers

B. Admission to telemetry for IV heparin and beta-blockers

C. Administration of an H2 blocker such as ranitidine

D. Placement of a temporary pacemaker for new left bundle branch block

E. Administration of lytics

QUESTION 88

Which of the following statements regarding diabetes mellitus is FALSE?

A. Patients with Type 1 DM are dependent on insulin.

B. Patients with Type 2 DM may have elevated insulin levels, especially early in the disease process.

C. Type 1 DM is more likely to run in families than Type 2 DM.

D. Type 2 DM develop DKA less frequently than Type 1 DM patients.

E. Patients with diabetes are prone to having high levels of triglycerides.

QUESTION 89

A 58-year-old female with a history of tobacco abuse and poorly controlled hypertension presents with a cough. Chest x-ray shows a large right-sided pleural effusion. Thoracentesis is performed with the following results:

Protein 5.5 mg/dl

LDH 250 U/L

Glucose 48

pH 7.30

Gram stain—no organisms

Serum LDH 140

Serum protein 7.8

Serum glucose 105

Which of the following is the *least* likely diagnosis?

A. Parapneumonic effusion with community acquired pneumonia

B. Rheumatoid arthritis

C. Small cell lung cancer

D. Congestive heart failure

E. Pulmonary tuberculosis

QUESTION 90

All of the following statements about chronic diarrhea are true EXCEPT:

A. Diarrhea is defined as an increase in stool weight above 200 g a day.

B. The four major pathogenic mechanisms for diarrhea are increased secretion, osmotic load, inflammation, and altered intestinal motility.

C. The stool osmotic gap is used to distinguish inflammatory diarrhea from secretary diarrhea.

D. The D-xylose test is used to evaluate osmotic diarrhea and measures the absorptive capacity of the proximal small bowel.

E. All of the above statements are true.

QUESTION 91

A 28-year-old male presents to the emergency department complaining of fevers and chills. On further questioning, he describes a 4-week history of intermittent fevers, a 10 kg weight loss and generalized fatigue. He states that he was told that he had a heart murmur during an employment physical several years prior. He has been otherwise healthy, and his only prior surgical procedure was extraction of his wisdom teeth approximately 6 weeks ago. He smokes a pack of cigarettes per day for the past 15 years but denies IV drug use or alcohol abuse. On physical exam, he is found to have a fever to 38.5°C (101.3°F) and heart rate of 110. Lung exam reveals some scattered crackles bilaterally, but cardiac exam reveals a III/VI systolic murmur radiating to the apex. He has no jugular venous distension or peripheral edema, but he has some small painless erythematous papules on his finger tips. Urinalysis is positive for 2+ protein. Chest x-ray reveals some bilateral patchy infiltrates. What is the most likely diagnosis?

A. Urinary tract infection

B. Community acquired pneumonia

C. Adenocarcinoma of the lung

D. Lymphoma

E. Subacute bacterial endocarditis

QUESTION 92

A 60-year-old male presents complaining of fatigue and a 7 kg weight loss over 5 months. He is quite concerned about worsening joint pain, especially in his wrists and fingers. He also reports some orthopnea and dyspnea on exertion. He tells you that he wakes up at night with pain and numbness in his right hand that improves with repeated wrist flexion and extension. Physical exam is significant for synovitis and swelling of the MCPS, PIPs, and wrists bilaterally. He has a positive Phalen's sign. Cardiopulmonary exam is significant for an S4, mild jugular venous distension, and bibasilar crackles. Extremities show 1-2+ pedal edema. He has good dentitia, but his tongue appears larger than normal. Chest x-ray shows mild cardiomegaly and pulmonary congestion, and EKG is shown. Which of the following tests is most likely to be diagnostic?

A. Biopsy of fat pad shows positive staining with Congo Red dye.

B. Aspiration of the wrist shows negatively birefringent, needle-shaped crystals.

C. Serum is positive for antibodies to double-stranded DNA.

D. Head CT shows an area of focal infarct.

E. Echocardiogram shows a large pericardial effusion with tamponade.

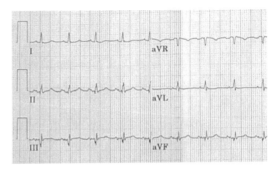

FIGURE 92

QUESTION 93

Which of the following statements regarding prosthetic valves is TRUE?

A. A mechanical valve in the aortic position does not require chronic anticoagulation.

B. The desired anticoagulation level with a mechanical valve in the mitral position is an INR of 1.5–2.5.

C. If a patient has a TIA from a cardiogenic source while on therapeutic levels of warfarin, it is acceptable to add low dose aspirin to the anticoagulation regimen.

D. A porcine or bioprosthetic valve lasts longer than a mechanical valve, but the risk of thromboembolism is higher with a porcine or bioprosthetic valve.

E. Patients with mechanical valves placed in the mitral position should have warfarin anticoagulation for 3 months, after which time they can be transitioned to aspirin as their sole anticoagulant medicine.

QUESTION 94

A 65-year-old patient with known advanced non-Hodgkin's lymphoma is admitted to the hospital lethargic and dehydrated. Lab evaluation reveals an elevated serum calcium of 13, moderate renal insufficiency, and a modest elevation of transaminases, bilirubin, and alkaline phosphatase. Which of the following statements is TRUE?

A. The serum PTH level should be suppressed.

B. The patient should receive large amounts of normal saline.

C. The patient's hypercalcemia will probably be steroid responsive.

D. The hypercalcemia associated with granulomatous disorders and lymphomas is mediated by a vitamin-related mechanism.

E. All of the above.

QUESTION 95

A 26-year-old previously healthy male presents complaining of a 5-day history of cough and fevers. He works as a radiology technician and does not smoke. Physical exam reveals that his respiratory rate is 22, pulse is 85, blood pressure is 110/72, and pulse oximetry is 93% on room air. He has rales in his right lower lung field with egophany in that area. Cardiac exam is normal, including good perfusion of the extremities. A chest x-ray is shown. Which of the following is the best therapy for this patient?

A. PO Amoxicillin-clavulenic acid (Augmentin)

B. IV Levofloxacin

C. PO Azithromycin

D. IV Cefuroxime

E. Wait for sputum culture results before beginning therapy

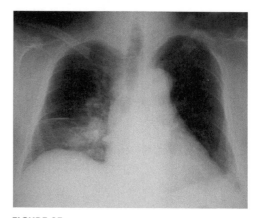

FIGURE 95

QUESTION 96

A 22-year-old white female presents with complaints of a 3- to 4-week history of joint pain, which involves both knees, her right ankle, left shoulder, and both hands. She has also noted a nonpruritic erythematous rash on her arms that is worse after being in the sun. She has had intermittent low-grade fevers. Physical exam reveals synovitis and effusions of the joints described, as well as the rash pictured. Cardiac exam reveals a II/VI systolic murmur at the left lower sternal border that does not radiate and decreases with valsalva. Urinalysis is positive for 2+ protein but no blood or leukocytes. CBC reveals a normocytic normochromic anemia. Which of the following is most likely to be positive?

A. Serum C-ANCA

B. Synovial fluid with gram positive cocci on gram stain

C. Echocardiogram with vegetations on the mitral valve

D. Serum anti-double stranded DNA antibody

E. High C3 and C4 serum complement levels

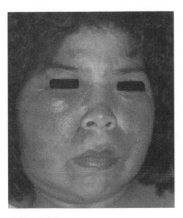

FIGURE 96

QUESTION 97

A 55-year-old man is admitted for chest pain and is subsequently diagnosed with an inferior wall myocardial infarction. On the second hospital day, the following rhythm strip was obtained. (See accompanying figure.) The patient is pain free. His blood pressure is 120/70. Which of the following statements is true?

A. This condition often leads to complete heart block and a pacemaker should be placed.

B. This is an example of second-degree AV block of Mobitz II type.

C. This condition should be treated with a Procainamide drip.

D. This condition does not require pacing unless hemodynamic problems are associated with a slow heart rate.

E. This condition represents blocked atrial premature contractions.

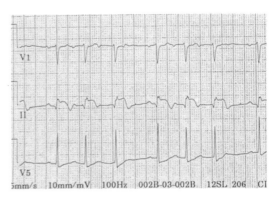

FIGURE 97

QUESTION 98

A 45-year-old woman is admitted for recurrent hypoglycemia. She was somewhat confused and had a glucose level of 32. Her symptoms and hypoglycemia corrected rapidly with infusion of 50% dextrose solution. Her history is positive for asymptomatic hepatitis C and fibromyalgia, but is negative for diabetes or other endocrine problems. She reports 5 or 6 episodes of hypoglycemia this year, and this is the second one documented by lab work. She states that the episodes usually occur 3–4 hr after eating a high carbohydrate meal. She drinks socially, and admits to occasionally having up to 4 drinks per day, in spite of counseling to abstain from alcohol in view of her hepatitis C. Family history is negative except for a son with Type 1 DM and a father who has Type 2 DM treated with a sulfonylurea. Labs drawn during admission include mild transaminase elevations, normal albumin and protime, elevated insulin levels, and a C-peptide level that is low. What is the most likely cause of her hypoglycemic episodes?

A. Insulinoma

B. Surreptitious insulin injection

C. Alcohol induced hypoglycemia

D. Adrenal insufficiency

E. Ingestion of oral hypoglycemics such as sulfonylureas

QUESTION 99

A 67-year-old previously healthy male presents with a 1-month history of worsening dyspnea. He also reports some right-sided chest discomfort that does not radiate and is not affected by exertion, motion, or deep breaths. He denies fever, chills, and cough. He is married and is a retired ship builder. He denies cigarette smoking. Chest x-ray shows a large right sided pleural effusion. EKG shows normal sinus rhythm with no ST-T abnormalities. A PPD skin test shows local erythema but no induration at 48 hr. Thoracentesis is performed and reveals bloody fluid consistent with an exudate, but cytology is negative. What is the most likely diagnosis?

A. Community acquired pneumonia with a parapneumonic effusion

B. Tuberculosis

C. Malignant mesothelioma

D. Small cell lung cancer with a malignant pleural effusion

E. Acute myocardial infarction with congestive heart failure

QUESTION 100

Each of the following is part of the classic pentad that comprises thrombotic thrombocytopenic purpura (TTP) EXCEPT:

A. Fever

B. Hemolytic anemia with spherocytes seen on peripheral smear

C. Thrombocytopenia

D. Decreased renal function

E. Confusion, delirium, or alteration of consciousness

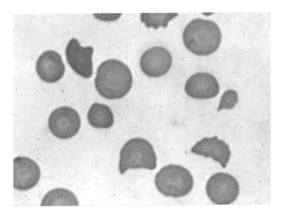

FIGURE 100

BLOCK **ONE**

ANSWERS

ANSWER 1

C. A ripping or tearing character of the pain, radiation to the back, abnormal x-ray, and a blood pressure differential in the arms are suggestive of dissecting aortic aneurysm. The patient's body habitus may suggest Marfan's syndrome, which is often associated with this diagnosis. The hands show very long fingers in an appearance known as arachnodactyly. The diastolic murmur is suggestive of aortic insufficiency, which can occur if the dissection involves the aortic valve. The most common etiology of dissecting aneurysm is hypertension and atherosclerosis.

A. MI is not associated with BP differential and may have ST segment elevation on EKG.

B. Unstable angina is not associated with a BP differential and often has ST segment depression on EKG.

D. PE is not associated with a BP differential, and the pain in embolus is often pleuritic in nature.

E. Pericarditis is not associated with a BP differential, and the pain of pericarditis is usually pleuritic.

ANSWER 2

E. This patient has Graves' disease, the most common cause of hyperthyroidism in America. While many of her findings are found in all forms of hyperthyroidism, the pre-tibial myxedema, lid puffiness, and exophthalmos are found only in Graves' disease. Graves' disease is an autoimmune disorder. Thyroid-stimulating immunoglobulin attaches to the thyroid follicle cell membrane, mimicking the actions of endogenous TSH. This leads to increased iodide uptake, overproduction of T_4 and T_3, and hyperthyroidism.

ANSWER 3

D. This patient most likely has a pulmonary embolus. Her chest pain was of sudden onset and is pleuritic in nature. It is accompanied by dyspnea, tachycardia, and tachypnea. Her oxygen saturation is also lower than would be expected with a clear chest x-ray. Her risk factors include smoking and estrogen use. A V/Q scan is the best first step in diagnosing a PE in a patient for whom the clinical suspicion is high.

A. Although this is also very reasonable to do in this patient with chest pain and shortness of breath, a V/Q scan would be the better study initially.

B. Immediate angiography would be inappropriate in this woman with atypical chest pain and no signs of ischemia on her EKG.

C. Appropriate treatment for PE (following diagnosis) would be to start either a heparin drip or low-molecular-weight heparin injections initially because warfarin takes at least 4–5 days to reach therapeutic levels. It is advisable, therefore, to start warfarin on the first day, but it must not be started without the simultaneous use of heparin.

E. It is inappropriate to give lytics in this patient with no EKG changes suggestive of infarct. Lytics may sometimes be used in a patient who is hemodynamically unstable because of a large pulmonary embolus. But this patient's blood pressure is stable, and her tachycardia is mild.

ANSWER 4

B. A perforated peptic ulcer is the most likely diagnosis in this patient who has a history of rheumatoid arthritis and who may be taking NSAIDs and steroids. She has signs of rebound tenderness (indicative of peritoneal inflammation), and a surgeon should be called to evaluate her promptly.

A. Patients who present with pancreatitis usually describe the pain as constant and radiating to the back. They usually do not have signs of peritoneal inflammation which directs you to a possible surgical problem, and they usually do not have evidence of gastrointestinal bleeding, such as coffee ground emesis and guaiac positive stools, unless a concomitant problem is occurring.

C. Esophageal varices develop because of portal hypertension usually related to cirrhotic liver disease. Patients whose varices bleed usually have gross hematemesis with bright red blood. They do not have signs of peritoneal inflammation, and the bleeding is usually painless.

D. Patients with a ruptured appendix may have peritoneal signs, but they usually also have a history of fever, anorexia, and diffuse nonlocalized abdominal pain which subsequently localizes to the right lower quadrant.

E. Ischemic bowel should be suspected in a patient who complains of severe pain out of proportion to physical exam. Patients at high risk for ischemic bowel are those with severe atherosclerotic vascular disease or atrial fibrillation with the potential for an embolus.

ANSWER 5

D. Iron deficiency anemia is associated with a *low* reticulocyte count. The problem is a lack of iron, which is one of the important building blocks needed to synthesize heme. Because of the lack of iron, the body is unable to produce blood cells in adequate number, and this includes the synthesis of reticulocytes. Reticulocytes are early red blood cells with residual ribosomal RNA still present.

A. Iron deficiency anemia is characterized by microcytic cells with a *low* mean corpuscular volume (MCV). As the iron stores become depleted, the cells produced become smaller due to the lack of hemoglobin. With worsening iron deficiency, erythropoietin levels become elevated and the resulting stimulation of the bone marrow causes cells to be produced that are bizarre in appearance and misshapen (poikilocytes). This is a sign of ineffective erythropoiesis.

B. The red cell distribution width (RDW) describes the uniformity of the red cells. A low number describes a very monomorphic cell population, whereas a high number describes a wide variety of cell shapes and sizes. In iron deficiency, the ineffective erythropoiesis results in a wide variety of cell shapes and sizes reflected in the *high* RDW.

C. Protoporphyrins combine with iron to form heme. Because of the lack of iron, the red cell protoporphyrins in the cell are increased. The average red cell protoporphyrin level is 30 μg/dl. The level rises quickly to greater than 100 μg/dl in iron deficiency anemia.

E. Serum ferritin is used to evaluate total body iron stores. Normal adult males have serum ferritin levels of 50–200 μg/l which correlates with 800 to 1000 mg or more of tissue iron stores. As iron stores are depleted, the serum ferritin falls. Levels of 15–20 μg/l or less indicate exhausted iron stores.

ANSWER 6

D. This patient most likely has an aspiration pneumonia, including anaerobic organisms. He aspirated oral flora a week ago when he passed out after drinking. The foul-smelling sputum and right-upper lobe location are classic for aspiration.

A. Toxoplasmosis causes tender lymphadenopathy, night sweats, and occasional CNS involvement. It is most often seen in immunocompromised patients.

B. Gram-negative organisms are an unlikely cause of pneumonia in this otherwise healthy young man.

C. Although pulmonary coccidiodomycosis cannot definitely be ruled out, it usually presents more indolently in healthy patients, and it is usually seen as a nonproductive cough, fatigue, and chest pain in patients who have traveled to Arizona or southern California.

E. Chemical pneumonitis is frequently seen after aspiration, but it would be seen within the first few days following the aspiration, not a week later.

ANSWER 7

E. The serum anion gap (AG) is a calculation which is defined as the difference between the unmeasured anions (UA) and the unmeasured cations (UC) in the serum. It is used to classify a metabolic acidosis so that the etiology of the acidosis may be identified. There are two types of metabolic acidosis: 1) increased anion gap and 2) normal anion gap, also called "non-anion gap." The anion gap principle is based on electroneutrality, which states that the number of positively charged ions and the number of negatively charged ions in a solution must be equal.

SUM OF ALL CATIONS = SUM OF ALL ANIONS

We measure only a few of the cations in serum, namely sodium and potassium. There are other unmeasured cations in the serum, including calcium, magnesium, and others. Similarly, we measure only a few of the anions in serum, namely chloride and bicarbonate. The unmeasured anions in serum include albumin, phosphate, sulfate, and other organic anions. Because of the above statement, we can conclude that:

Sum of measured cations + Sum of unmeasured cations = Sum of measured anions + Sum of unmeasured anions

By rearranging the above equation, we can conclude that:

Sum of measured cations – Sum of measured anions = Sum of unmeasured anions – Sum of unmeasured cations

Replacing the second half of the equation with ANION GAP (its definition), we see that:

$$(Na^+ + K^+) - (Cl^- + HCO_3^-) = AG$$

Because of the small magnitude of changes in potassium concentration, potassium is usually omitted from the equation.

The anion gap is a convenient tool that helps a clinician estimate whether there has been a change in the unmeasured anions or cations even before a change can be documented by direct measurements. Normal anion gap is 14 ± or –2 mEq/L. Increases in the anion gap are caused by the addition of a non-chloride containing acid such as lactate, salicylic acid, ketoacids, or in uremia. Isopropyl alcohol (rubbing alcohol) is metabolized by alcohol dehydrogenase to the end products of acetone, carbon dioxide, and water. It produces an osmolar gap and ketosis without a significant metabolic acidosis.

ANSWER 8

D. This patient has a classic case of sarcoidosis. It is most common in black females. The clinical manifestations typically include a dry cough, arthralgias, and systemic symptoms including fever, weight loss, and fatigue. Erythema nodosum is also frequently seen in patients with sarcoid.

A. Goodpasture's disease is an autoimmune disease causing hemoptysis, anemia and diffuse pulmonary infiltrates along with glomerulonephritis.

B. Histoplasmosis is a fungal infection that is usually subclinical. But in an immunocompromised patient, it may present with pulmonary infiltrates as well as skin and bone marrow involvement.

C. Although she has both arthritis and symptoms of pleural inflammation, this patient does not have enough symptoms to meet criteria for SLE.

E. Lung cancer can cause weight loss and pulmonary symptoms, but it does not cause arthralgias or erythema nodosum. Also, this patient is quite young to have lung cancer from her smoking.

ANSWER 9

A. This patient's age and prostate cancer put him at high risk for pulmonary embolism. The presentation of dyspnea and pleuritic chest pain is not unusual, and many patients have tachypnea, tachycardia, and a low grade fever. The paucity of diagnostic findings makes a high index of suspicion important. Less than 50% of those with a pulmonary embolus have leg findings, and hemoptysis is a classic but fairly unusual finding. The loud P2 is caused by a sudden increase in pulmonary pressures. A V/Q scan is a well-accepted first step in diagnosing a pulmonary embolism.

B. The pleuritic nature of his pain and lack of any EKG findings make an acute coronary syndrome less likely.

C. Lack of cough or infiltrate make pneumonia unlikely even though patient has dyspnea and fever.

D. An echo may show signs of pulmonary hypertension but would not be appropriate as a first test to rule out PE.

E. D-dimer shows some promise as a marker of thromboembolism but does not have sufficient sensitivity or specificity to be used as a reliable marker to rule out this potentially fatal disorder.

ANSWER 10

D. DeQuervain's thyroiditis is a granulomatous painful thyroiditis that is probably caused by a viral infection. This entity commonly has a viral prodrome and may be associated with fevers. There is characteristically severe tenderness of the thyroid gland. The transient hyperthyroidism associated with subacute thyroiditis is caused by a damaged gland that leaks thyroid hormone, not by an overactive thyroid. Radioactive iodine uptake is diminished in DeQuervain's thyroiditis and other forms of subacute thyroiditis.

A. Graves presents with painless goiter and increased radioactive iodine uptake. This patient has no proptosis, skin findings, or eye findings specific to Graves' disease.

B. This patient should have low iodine uptake.

C. Hashimoto's is a chronic lymphocytic thyroiditis that is associated with a painless goiter. This is a common cause of hypothyroidism and is expected to have a low iodine uptake.

E. See the explanation for 'A' above.

ANSWER 11

C. This patient has cystic fibrosis. She was born with a meconium ileus, which is common in patients born with CF. She has had recurrent bouts of respiratory infections because of the pulmonary component of the disease. Now she has malabsorption secondary to pancreatic insufficiency, a common complication of CF.

A. This is not an infectious process. Although an intestinal parasite can cause diarrhea and weight loss, the oily, foul-smelling stools are classic for malabsorption. The fact that the diarrhea gets better when the patient fasts further suggests malabsorption.

B. One cannot definitively rule out inflammatory bowel disease or bacterial overgrowth of the large bowel, which could both be diagnosed by colonoscopy. However, in this patient with no history of melena or hematochezia and the history of meconium ileus and respiratory infections, cystic fibrosis with pancreatic insufficiency is a more likely diagnosis.

D. This patient does not have immunodeficiency; her respiratory infections were caused by an inability to mobilize mucous.

E. *H. pylori* causes duodenal and gastric ulcers, not diarrhea.

ANSWER 12

A. This patient has ulcerative colitis by history and biopsy. Patients with 10 years of active disease are at extremely high risk of developing colon cancer. During the course of their disease, they should be screened with colonoscopy every one to two years depending on the severity of their clinical course.

B. Antibiotics are used in the treatment of Crohn's disease but have no proven benefit in ulcerative colitis.

C. Complications of ulcerative colitis include toxic megacolon and colon carcinoma. Complications of Crohn's disease include bowel obstruction and fistula formation.

D. The skin lesions seen in association with inflammatory bowel disease are pyoderma gangrenosum and erythema nodosum. This patient has a classic pyoderma gangrenosum that has an association with ulcerative colitis. PG is ulcerative with a violaceous border. Erythema nodosum is a raised painful erythematous nodule most often seen on the anterior calf.

E. Inflammatory bowel diseases occur more often in whites than in blacks, and more often in men than in women.

ANSWER 13

D. Autoimmune hemolytic anemia may present with an acute or chronic anemia. If the MCV is elevated in hemolytic anemia, it is usually because the reticulocyte count is high and the early larger red cell precursors are being pushed into the circulation by the hyperstimulated bone marrow. These early large cells artificially elevate the MCV. The patient presented here has a low corrected reticulocyte count with a high MCV which is more indicative of a macrocytic anemia, *not* a hemolytic anemia. A reticulocyte index of greater than 3% is more indicative of shortened red cell survival and stimulated bone marrow as in autoimmune hemolytic anemia.

A. This patient has a macrocytic anemia. The most common etiologies are folate deficiency and vitamin B^{12} deficiency. Alcohol abusers, whose caloric intake is derived mostly from alcohol, are at risk of folate deficiency because of a poor diet, and because alcohol directly interferes with folate metabolism.

B. Drugs that cause megaloblastic anemia do so by interfering with DNA synthesis directly or by antagonizing the action of folate. Methotrexate is a chemotherapeutic agent that works by inhibiting dihydrofolate reductase and therefore inhibiting DNA synthesis, causing a megaloblastic, macrocytic anemia.

C. Hypothyroidism is a cause of macrocytic anemia. It is thought to be related to the autoimmune process and the fact that pernicious anemia occurs in approximately 12% of patients with autoimmune mediated primary hypothyroidism.

E. Dysplastic anemias are primary stem cell disorders, many of which eventually evolve to acute leukemia. They are a source of low reticulocyte count macrocytic anemias.

ANSWER 14

C. *Pneumocystis carinii* pneumonia typically shows diffuse bilateral infiltrates. Lymphadenopathy is uncommon.

A. Tuberculosis typically involves lymphadenopathy, occasionally in the absence of other obvious radiographic findings.

B. Lymphoma can present initially as hilar adenopathy.

D. Any fungal pulmonary infection can cause lymphadenopathy.

E. Sarcoid typically presents as bilateral hilar adenopathy with fevers.

ANSWER 15

A. The clinical manifestations of hyponatremia are largely neurologic and reflect the brain edema from osmotic water shifts in the brain. Significant symptoms do not usually appear until the serum sodium is less than 125 mEq/L, and the severity of the symptoms can be roughly correlated with the degree of hypoosmolality. The rapidity of the onset of the hypoosmolality, the pre-existence of neurological problems, and the presence of other non-neurologic metabolic disturbances all can affect the degree of symptoms that a patient has with any given level of serum osmolality. Thiazide diuretics used in higher doses may cause significant electrolyte abnormalities such as hyponatremia and hypokalemia. An electrolyte panel should be obtained 1 week after starting a diuretic for hypertension to watch for electrolyte disturbances.

B. Hypernatremia results when there is net water loss or hypertonic sodium gain. Patients with acute severe hypernatremia may experience brain shrinkage and the traction that results on the intracerebral veins may cause them to rupture and bleed. The manifestations of less severe hypernatremia are nonspecific and include nausea, muscle weakness, and alterations in mental status. Seizures are rare.

C. Hyperkalemia results in cardiac rhythm disturbances and possibly cardiac arrest. Severe hyperkalemia can cause skeletal muscle weakness to the point of paralysis and respiratory failure. Neurologic symptoms are not a prominent feature of potassium disturbances.

D. Hypokalemia can occur with thiazide diuretic use. It may result in electrocardiographic changes and ventricular arrhythmias in patients with ischemic heart disease or in patients taking digoxin. Severe hypokalemia is associated with variable degrees of skeletal muscle weakness to the point of paralysis and respiratory failure. Rarely, it may cause rhabdomvolvsis.

ANSWER 16

C. This patient has the typical migratory asymmetric arthritis and diffuse tenosynovitis seen with systemic gonococcal infection. The rash described is also typical for gonococcus.

A. Rheumatoid arthritis is a symmetric arthritis, typically involving at least three joints and usually involving the hands. The rash does not support a diagnosis of RA.

B. Monoarthritis secondary to calcium pyrophosphate crystals does frequently involve the knee. However, it would be unusual in someone so young with no associated medical problems. It does not involve a rash.

D. Fibromyalgia is a syndrome involving specific areas of point tenderness accompanied by general symptoms of fatigue and myalgias and arthralgias.

E. Although Lyme disease may cause an asymmetric pauciarticular arthritis, the rash seen is that of erythema migrans, and the rash precedes the arthritis.

ANSWER 17

E. Coronary disease is the most common cause of adult US deaths, even after more than 20 years of improvement in the mortality rate; 500,000 deaths per year are attributed to this process in spite of advances in prevention and treatment.

A, B, C, and D are far less common causes of mortality than coronary disease.

ANSWER 18

E. This patient is probably taking some of her daughter's exogenous thyroid replacement. Health care workers and women attempting to accelerate weight loss are the most likely to abuse thyroid replacement medications. There is no goiter and the iodine uptake is reduced.

A, B, and C are not consistent with this patient's presentation. Toxic multinodular goiter, hyperthyroidism secondary to a TSH secreting tumor, and Graves' disease would all have high iodine uptake on a thyroid scan and goiters. Answer B is also incorrect because the TSH would obviously be high, instead of low as in this case.

D. Subacute thyroiditis is the only other answer listed above that is associated with reduced iodine uptake on thyroid scan. The absence of autoimmune antibodies and her patient profile makes exogenous ingestion of thyroid hormone more likely.

ANSWER 19

B. This is a morbidly obese patient (BMI = 41.5) with a crowded oropharynx and snoring. He most likely has obstructive sleep apnea with frequent nighttime awakenings and resultant daytime somnolence.

A. This patient does not have cataplexy or hypnagogic hallucinations. He did not describe sleep paralysis. Therefore this patient does not have three of the four components of narcolepsy.

C. This patient is classic for OSA, and primary snoring would not account for his daytime somnolence.

D. Although his elderly mother likely has restless leg syndrome, this is much more common in the elderly and in pregnant women.

E. This patient's sleep habits are actually fairly good. He goes to sleep and wakes up at the same time each day, and he doesn't wake up at night. He does not use excessive alcohol, caffeine or other drugs that affect sleep.

ANSWER 20

D. Testicular *atrophy*, not testicular enlargement, occurs in patients with chronic liver disease. This is because of an increase in circulating estrogens. With liver failure, the liver is unable to clear estrogens from the blood and the ratio of estrogen to free testosterone goes up.

A. Spider angiomas are commonly seen in patients with chronic liver disease. They are most common on the face, neck, and upper chest. They are thought to be due to excess estrogen or the increased ratio of estrogen to free testosterone. Spider angiomas may also be seen in pregnant women and in women taking oral contraceptives.

B. Hemorrhoids are not specific for liver disease but may indicate portal hypertension and a resulting increase in blood flow and pressure in collateral veins such as the esophageal veins (varices), the superficial abdominal wall (caput medusa), and the rectum (internal hemorrhoids).

C. Splenomegaly is seen in patients with significant portal hypertension because the splenic vein empties into the portal vein. When the flow of blood in the portal vein is impeded by high resistance, such as in cirrhosis, blood builds up in the spleen and enlargement of the spleen occurs.

E. Palmar erythema also may be seen in chronic liver disease, and this is also thought to secondary to high estrogen levels.

ANSWER 21

The distinguishing feature of all hemolytic anemias is the increased rate of mature red blood
cell destruction. The signs and symptoms differ
with the mechanism of the hemolysis as well
as the acuteness or chronicity of the red cell
destruction. The mechanism of destruction can
involve environmental factors such as mechanical heart valves, infection, or autoimmune attack.
Destruction may also occur to red cells with
abnormal membrane structures, hemoglobin
stability, or metabolic function, such as in hereditary spherocytosis, sickle cell disease, and
G-6-PD deficiency, respectively. The diagnosis of
hemolytic anemia depends heavily on laboratory findings.

E. Haptoglobin is the protein carrier that
binds to free hemoglobin. This complex is
then cleared by the liver. In both extravas-
cular and intravascular hemolysis, the
measured haptoglobin is LOW because it
is "used up."

A. The corrected reticulocyte count is measured by the formula:

Corrected retic count = Retic count ×
Patient's hematocrit/Expected
hematocrit

A corrected reticulocyte content of >3–5%
suggests early destruction and high red cell
turnover. Some patients may have corrected reticulocyte counts of 20% or higher.
A low corrected reticulocyte count (<2%)
suggests a primary bone marrow problem,
or a bone marrow that is unable to replace
red cells appropriately because of the lack
of "building blocks" as in iron deficiency
anemia.

B. An elevated LDH is seen in hemolytic
anemia because of the release of lactate
dehydrogenase from the lysed cells.

C. Spherocytes may be seen on the peripheral
smear of a patient with acquired hemolytic
anemia, such as in Coombs positive autoimmune destruction, splenomegaly due to
liver cirrhosis, and clostridial infections as
well as in certain snake envenomations.

D. The indirect bilirubin is elevated in hemolysis because the liver's ability to conjugate
the bilirubin produced by the breakdown of
hemoglobin is overwhelmed.

ANSWER 22

B. Cough is not generally associated with
streptococcal pharyngitis. In a patient presenting with a sore throat and cough, the
differential diagnosis includes viral pharyngitis, gonococcal pharyngitis, sinusitis, and
acute FHV.

A. Anterior cervical lymph nodes are classically enlarged and tender in a patient with
streptococcal pharyngitis.

C. Fever is common in Group A Streptococcal
infections involving the throat.

D. Headache is also commonly seen in association with strep throat.

E. Strep pharyngitis typically involves large
red tonsils with exudates. However, some
cases of viral pharyngitis can also involve
exudates, so this is not definitive.

ANSWER 23

D. Nephrolithiasis has an annual incidence of 7–21 cases per 10,000 persons in the United States. Men are affected four times more often than women with nephrolithiasis in general, but each type of stone has a "sex preference." Seventy-five percent of stones are calcium oxalate, and they affect more men than women. Their pathogenesis may be idiopathic, or patients may have a variety of urinary abnormalities such as low urine volume, hypercalcuria, hyperoxaluria, or hypocitraturia. After a first calcium stone, 40% of untreated patients will have another stone within 5 years.

A. Uric acid stones occur in two circumstances: excessive urinary uric acid excretion and persistently acidic urine. These stones have an equal incidence between men and women and are radiolucent on x-ray. Our patient's stone was radioopaque.

B. Struvite stones are more common in women and are caused by urinary infections with certain bacteria like *Proteus* or *Providencia* species. These bacteria cleave urea to ammonia and thereby elevate the urine pH to 8 or greater. This favors the precipitation of struvite and apatite. Struvite stones are the second most common stones after calcium stones. They make up 15–20% of all stones.

C. Cystine stones account for only 1% of all kidney stones. They usually result from an unusual inherited disorder in which renal tubular absorption of cystine, ornithine, arginine, and lysine (COAL) is reduced. They have an equal incidence in men and women. These stones are rare, and our patient has a much higher probability of having a calcium oxalate stone.

ANSWER 24

B. The rhomboid, positively birefringent crystals are calcium pyrophosphate. This patient's pseudogout may be related to his hypothyroidism.

A. The uric acid crystals of gout are needle-shaped and negatively birefringent.

C. This patient's WBC count in the synovial fluid is high enough to suggest a septic joint, but the crystals point to pseudogout.

D. Rheumatoid arthritis is a symmetric arthritis involving more than three joints and usually involving the hands.

E. Although the patient is on coumadin, there is no evidence that he bled into his knee.

ANSWER 25

D. This patient has a classic presentation for acute myocardial infaction. Most cases are caused by plaque rupture and thrombus formation, which is why antiplatelet agents and thrombolytics are beneficial in many cases. Most culprit atherosclerotic lesions causing infarction are occlusive of less than 50% of the artery prior to the infarct.

A. Incorrect for the reasons stated above. This kind of lesion may be associated with stable angina.

B. Spasm can cause angina and infarct, but is a far less common cause of infarct than plaque rupture, and would be more likely women without such pronounced atherosclerotic risk factors.

C. This clinical picture is not consistent with pericarditis. Pericarditis causes positional pleuritic pain. While it can be associated with ST-segment elevation, these changes would not generally be limited to the anteroseptal leads.

E. Aortic aneurysms can extend into the coronary arteries and cause infarction, but there is no ripping or tearing pain with radiation in this case. Aneurysm dissection is an uncommon mechanism of infarction.

ANSWER 26

B. A serum T_3 is needed to rule out T_3 thyrotoxicosis. In this condition, hyperthyroidism is caused by the bio-active T_3 while T_4 is normal.

A. This test is used to screen for adrenal insufficiency.

C. This patient has clinical hyperthyroidism and a low TSH suggesting primary hyperthyroidism. If the patient had hypothyroidism and a low TSH, we would get a sella imaging study to rule out empty sella syndrome or other destructive pituitary conditions. It might also be appropriate to obtain a sella imaging study if the patient had an elevated TSH with hyperthyroidism, leading you to suspect a pituitary tumor secreting TSH inappropriately.

D. Thyroid binding globulin (TBG) would not rule out T_3 thyrotoxicosis and is not needed when you measure free T_4 levels.

ANSWER 27

E. Inhaled steroids are good maintenance medications for asthma. Daily use of inhaled steroids has been shown to improve symptoms and decrease hospitalizations. This patient has sufficiently frequent symptoms to warrant the addition of inhaled steroids to her daily regimen.

A. When used correctly, nebulized albuterol is no more effective than a metered-dose inhaler. However, during an acute attack sometimes tachypnea can prevent a patient from being able to use an MDI properly.

B. Systemic steroids should be reserved for acute attacks.

C. Theophylline would not generally be added before an inhaled steroid because of its considerable side effects.

D. The beta agonists should be used only as often as is needed to keep symptoms under control.

ANSWER 28

D. Metformin is an oral medication used in the treatment of diabetes type 2. Its most concerning side effect is a development of lactic acidosis. Its main gastrointestinal side effects are bloating and mild abdominal discomfort, but not pancreatitis. Drugs associated with pancreatitis include azathioprine, thiazides, furosemide, estrogens, and dideoxyinosine (ddI).

A. Ethanol ingestion is one of the leading causes of pancreatitis.

B. Gallstones that partially pass through the common bile duct and obstruct the pancreatic duct are the next leading cause of pancreatitis. This patient has a history suggestive of biliary colic with right upper quadrant pain and shoulder pain associated with fatty meals. She is also at high risk for gallstones being "female, forty, fertile, and obese."

C. Hypertriglyceridemia is associated with pancreatitis, and this patient may have high triglycerides related to her diabetes and insulin resistance. Usually, the triglycerides are over a thousand before pancreatitis develops, and patients with diabetes mellitus type 2 often only have a mild elevation of triglycerides.

E. Pancreas divisum is a congenital abnormality of the pancreas that predisposes patients to pancreatitis. It is significantly less common than alcohol or gallstone pancreatitis.

ANSWER 29

A. This patient has chronic lymphocytic leukemia. It is a disease of older adults (90% over 40 years), and its major clinical manifestation is an increase in the number of circulating lymphocytes. It may present in an asymptomatic patient with an increased number of lymphocytes on peripheral smear, and the fragile malignant cells may "smudge" on preparation of the smear. Patients may have minimal to massive lymphadenopathy. Other symptoms include malaise, easy fatigability, weight loss, and night sweats. In the Americas and in Europe, the most common form of CLL is of B-cell origin. With marrow involvement, patients may develop anemia, thrombocytopenia, or pancytopenia. Patients are often hypogammaglobulinemic and may present with recurrent bacterial infections due to encapsulated organisms. Other immunologic phenomena may occur including Coombs positive hemolytic anemia and immune-mediated thrombocytopenia. The immunophenotyping shows the presence of CD5, and there is a low amount of surface immunoglobulin on the cell.

B. Chronic myelogenous leukemia is a myeloproliferative disorder, in which there is a dramatic increase in the number of mature and immature myelocytes in circulation and tissues. It is due to a chromosomal aberration; the 9;22 translocation called the Philadelphia chromosome. This seems to prevent cell death by aptoptosis of myeloid cells. Our patient has 70% mature lymphocytes on the smear which is not consistent with CML.

C. There are two peaks in the incidence of ALL; one in children less than 10 years old and the much smaller peak in adults over 50 years old. The onset is usually abrupt with no prodromal symptoms. Patients complain of weakness, bleeding, and infections. On laboratories, they may have a severe anemia, thrombocytopenia, and high white blood cell count with lymphoblasts predominant. Our patient has mature appearing lymphocytes predominating her blood smear with a chronic presentation of symptoms.

D. Acute myelogenous leukemia is a clonal proliferation of immature myeloid cells in the marrow and blood. It can present as an acute catastrophic illness or as a final outcome of other myeloproliferative diseases like CML, polycythemia vera, and myelofibrosis. Our patient, again, does not have blasts in her blood to suggest an acute leukemia.

E. Hairy cell leukemia is a type of lymphocyte malignancy similar to CLL; however, the malignant lymphocytes have long filamentous cytoplasmic projections that look like hair. They are seen in wet mount and tartrate-resistant acid phosphatase stain can be used to confirm the presence of hairy cells in circulation. Massive splenomegaly is common. Hairy cell leukemia responds well to interferon therapy.

ANSWER 30

C. This patient has HIV risk factors and oral thrush without other causes for an immuno-compromised state, so HIV is likely. His hypoxia, diffuse pulmonary infiltrates and insidious onset of nonproductive cough are classic findings in *Pneumocystis carinii* pneumonia. PCP is a common cause of hypoxic pneumonia in HIV positive patients. A high LDH is also suggestive of PCP.

A. Although HIV positive patients can sometimes have pulmonary TB with a negative skin test (anergy), this patient does not have hemoptysis or radiologic findings (like apical disease and hilar adenopathy) that are classically seen with tuberculosis.

B. This patient has no clinical findings (like JVD, pleural effusions, or a gallop) consistent with CHF.

D. Strep pneumonia is the most common cause of community acquired bacterial pneumonia. However, it usually causes a lobar infiltrate, not diffuse bilateral infiltrates.

E. Klebsiella most often causes an aspiration pneumonia in alcoholics.

ANSWER 31

E. Autosomal dominant polycystic kidney disease (ADPKD) is the most common hereditary renal disease and one of the most common hereditary diseases in this country. It affects 1:400 to 1:1000 Americans, and is the fourth most common cause of end stage renal disease. There are at least three different genetic abnormalities that can produce the disorder. It is not just a renal disease but a systemic disorder. There are many extrarenal manifestations as mentioned above.

ANSWER 32

D. This patient had a Baker's cyst behind her right knee that ruptured. A ruptured Baker's cyst (which is relatively common in rheumatoid arthritis) may mimic a DVT. An ultrasound will show the ruptured cyst. A doppler ultrasound would also diagnose a proximal DVT.

A. It is inappropriate to begin heparin prior to diagnosis in this patient who may not have a DVT.

B. This patient has no symptoms of a pulmonary embolus.

C. There is no reason to stop this patient's methotrexate.

E. Venography is not superior to ultrasound in diagnosing DVT, and it will not diagnose a Baker's cyst.

ANSWER 33

D. This woman has a classic presentation for mitral stenosis. Mitral stenosis is almost always caused by rheumatic heart disease. An opening snap is missing in this patient, probably because the valve has calcified and is no longer pliable. Patients can also present with hemoptysis, right-sided failure signs such as ascites and peripheral edema, and EKG signs of pulmonary hypertension. Mitral stenosis can induce atrial fibrillation, often with a rapid deterioration of cardiopulmonary reserve. She is still in sinus rhythm as we can tell by the regular rhythm and presystolic accentuation of the diastolic murmur.

A. Dilated cardiomyopathy is more likely to present with a large heart, left-sided failure signs, and an S3.

B. Aortic stenosis is in the differential for systolic (not diastolic) murmurs.

C. HOCM is in the differential for systolic (not diastolic) murmurs.

E. A bounding, collapsing pulse with wide pulse pressures (Corrigan's pulse) and a diastolic decrescendo murmur would be more characteristic of aortic regurgitation.

ANSWER 34

D. A patient with central hypothyroidism is not stimulating the thyroid gland with TSH which lowers the T_4 level. There is no goiter and the thyroid may be nonpalpable. Since the main problem is with the pituitary, antimicrosomal antibodies marking autoimmune problems with the thyroid are not usually found. Note that patients with central hypothyoidism need to be evaluated for other hormone deficiencies of hypopituitarism. If cortisol deficiency is found, cortisol replacement should be given before thyroid replacement to avoid acute adrenal insufficiency.

A, B, C, and E are all incorrect for the reasons stated above. Note also that E is incorrect because T_4 is expected to be low and serum T_3 levels are not helpful in the diagnosis of hypothyroidism. T_3 may be low in euthyroid patients with a variety of nonthyroidal illnesses and may be normal in a patient with hypothyroidism.

ANSWER 35

C. Calcifications in a solitary pulmonary nodule in a "popcorn" pattern suggests a benign hamartoma. Calcifications in a "bulls eye" or multiple punctuate calcifications are also usually benign.

A. A smoking history is a risk factor for cancer for at least 20 years after smoking cessation.

B. A nodule that is unchanged from two years ago is more likely to be a benign granuloma. In pulmonary nodules that are growing, malignancy needs to be considered. This is why it is important to look at old x-rays if they are available.

D. Although it is conceivable that the mass might be reactivated TB, lung cancer is more likely. Remember that 35% of solitary pulmonary nodules are malignant.

E. Hilar adenopathy is not always evident with pulmonary malignancies.

ANSWER 36

The serum-ascites albumin gradient (SAAG) is calculated by subtracting the albumin concentration of the ascites fluid from the serum albumin concentration. (Example: 4.0 g/dl – 2.5 g/dl = 1.5 g/dl.) The serum-ascites albumin gradient correlates directly with portal pressure. Patients with gradients *greater* than 1.1 g/dl have portal hypertension as a cause of their ascites. (Think of the old term, "transudate.") The high hydrostatic pressure seen in portal hypertension causes the accumulation of fluid in the peritoneal cavity. Patients with gradients *less* than 1.1 do not have portal hypertension. (Think of the old term, "exudate.") Portal hypertension is *not* the cause of this ascites, but rather some insult to the tissues that causes a leakage of fluid and proteins into the peritoneal cavity. Now, we can evaluate the choices above and choose the etiology of ascites that is *not* associated with portal hypertension.

E. Peritoneal carcinomatosis most often occurs secondary to adenocarcinomas of the ovary, pancreas, and colon. Ascites formation in these patients occurs because of increased capillary permeability and obstruction of the subdiaphragmatic lymphatics. In this case, the serum-ascites albumin gradient is less than 1.1.

A. Liver cirrhosis causes portal hypertension and high pressures in the collateral veins that drain into the portal vein. Therefore, esophageal varices, splenomegaly, caput medusa and internal hemorrhoids develop.

B. Congestive heart failure also causes a backflow of blood into the hepatic and portal vasculature and may cause an increase in portal pressure significant enough to cause portal hypertension ("cardiac ascites").

C. Budd–Chiari syndrome (thrombosis of the hepatic vein) also causes portal hypertension and ascites. This may occur in patients with abdominal trauma, patients taking birth control pills, or in patients with hematologic diseases and hypercoagulable states such as polycythemia vera.

D. Portal vein thrombosis obviously would cause portal hypertension. This may occur in patients following abdominal trauma or intra-abdominal sepsis, or in patients with cirrhosis or hepatocellular carcinoma.

ANSWER 37

E. Thrombocytopenia can occur because of inadequate production of platelets, sequestration of platelets in an enlarged spleen, or premature destruction of platelets in the circulation. A platelet has a lifespan of 9–10 days and therefore 15,000–45,000 platelets need to be produced each day to maintain a steady state.

Defects or reductions of marrow megakaryocyte mass (platelet precursor cells in the bone marrow) can occur because of radiation damage, cancer chemotherapy, exposure to toxins such as benzene or insecticides, or drugs such as alcohol. Marrow infiltration by cancers, infections, or fibrosis will frequently produce a platelet production defect.

Splenomegaly by itself should not reduce the platelet count to below 40,000–50,000. Patients may have a combination of immune-mediated thrombocytopenia along with a large spleen such as in ITP, and splenectomy may be beneficial therapy. Patients with chronic liver disease, however, like our patient, with splenomegaly due to portal hypertension, do not benefit from splenectomy.

There are many drugs associated with the development of thrombocytopenia. Heparin is one of the most commonly known drugs that can cause an autoimmune thrombocytopenia *and* a tendency for thrombosis. Heparin must be stopped immediately if the platelet count starts to fall while the patient is on the drug. Other drugs associated with thrombocytopenia include H_2 blockers, thiazides, estrogens, sulfonarnides, indomethacin.

In our patient, any of the three etiologies could be considered either alone or together as an etiology of his thrombocytopenia.

ANSWER 38

D. This patient has classic symptoms of bacterial meningitis. *Neisseria meningiditis* classically can give ischemic skin lesions. It is transmitted by respiratory secretions, so close social contacts should be given rifampin prophylaxis to prevent infection. This patient should be started on IV antibiotics immediately and have a lumbar puncture as soon as possible.

A. Although HSV is among the most common causes of viral encephalitis, it rarely causes the skin findings described in this patient.

B. Listeria causes meningitis in infants and the elderly, but not in young healthy persons.

C. Alcohol intoxication would not cause fever or nuchal rigidity.

E. Tertiary syphilis can cause neuro findings, including confusion and tabes dorsalis. But it does not have such an acute onset or high fevers.

ANSWER 39

C. When proteinuria is severe, it causes the nephrotic syndrome. The nephrotic syndrome is characterized by massive proteinuria (greater than 3 g of protein/24 hr), serum hypoalbuminemia, edema, hyperlipidemia, and lipiduria, represented by oval fat bodies. The two most common causes of nephrotic syndrome are minimal change disease (in children) and diabetes glomerulosclerosis (in adults). Severe nephrotic syndrome predisposes to *thrombosis* (not bleeding), because of the loss of protein C and S in the urine. It also may predispose patients to infection secondary to a loss of immunoglobulins and may predispose to atherosclerosis because of the hyperlipidemia. The liver tries to synthesize albumin to replace that which is lost in the urine, but the liver becomes confused and kicks out cholesterol which causes the hyperlipidemia.

ANSWER 40

C. Rheumatoid arthritis does not involve the DIP joints. However, the PIPs and MCPs are very frequently involved. RA typically is a symmetric arthritis that includes morning stiffness of more than an hour.

A. NSAIDs are a very important part of managing the pain of RA.

B. Rheumatoid nodules are one of the diagnostic criteria of RA.

D. This is a typical radiologic finding in a patient with RA.

E. Felty's syndrome consists of rheumatoid arthritis and splenomegaly and leukopenia.

ANSWER 41

B. This patient has a systolic murmur characteristic of aortic stenosis. The most likely etiology in a patient less than 55 is a congenital bicuspid aortic valve, which occurs in about 1% of the population. Characteristic are the distribution of this systolic murmur and the *pulsus parvus et tardus*. Bicuspid aortic stenosis can be associated with coarctation of the aorta, but this patient's blood pressure readings and lack of symptoms make this unlikely.

A. The Valsalva maneuver decreases preload. This makes the murmur of valvular AS less pronounced, while accentuating the murmur of HOCM. HOCM also is known for a brisk carotid upstroke that is bifid in two-thirds of patients.

C. Degeneration and calcification of a tricuspid aortic valve is more common in patients older than 55, whereas in younger patients a congenitally bicuspid valve is more common.

D. Mitral regurgitation causes a systolic murmur with a different distribution and is not associated with *pulsus parvus et tardus*.

E. Mitral stenosis is associated with a diastolic murmur.

ANSWER 42

A. Hashimoto's is associated with antiperoxidase antibodies in high titer 95% of the time. Antithyroglobulin antibodies are present in 55–60%. There is also an association with other autoimmune conditions such as vitiligo, Addison's disease, and pernicious anemia.

B. Hashimoto's can rarely present as hyperthyroidism, but most commonly presents with a euthyroid or hypothyroid goiter.

C. Thyroid scans would show a diminished iodine uptake.

D. While the goiter is often diffuse, Hashimoto's can present with nodular or multinodular goiter.

E. Hashimoto's is a condition most common in middle-aged and elderly populations. It is more common in women.

ANSWER 43

E. This patient has developed a tension Pneumothorax on the right side secondary to high ventilatory pressures. This is why he has the absence of breath sounds on the right. Left-sided tracheal deviation is due to increased right-sided intrathoracic pressure from the air in the pleural space.

A. A nosocomial pneumonia would not account for this sudden change in the patient's status or the tracheal deviation.

B. A worsening of the asthma could cause diminished to absent breath sounds, but would not likely present so acutely, nor would it cause tracheal deviation.

C. A mucous plug, either in the ETT or a bronchus, could cause a sudden worsening in respiratory status, but it would not explain this patient's physical exam findings.

D. If the patient had atelectasis, the trachea should be deviated *toward* the side of diminished breath sounds.

ANSWER 44

C. The consumption of saccharine sweeteners has been associated with an increased risk of bladder cancer in rats (not humans) and has not been associated with colon cancer.

A. A history of adenomatous polyps increases the risk of colon cancer; however, less than 5% of adenomas develop into carcinomas. There are three important factors that help predict the risk of transformation to cancer. These factors are size, histologic type, and epithelial dysplasia. A polyp less than 1 cm has a 1–3% risk of developing into cancer, whereas a polyp greater than 2 cm has a 40% risk of developing into cancer. The histologic types of tubular, tubulovillous, and villous neoplasms have an increasing risk of cancer occurrence in that order. The degree of dysplasia is evaluated by the pathologist reading the biopsy slide.

B. Patients with both Crohn's disease and ulcerative colitis (UC) have an increased risk of colon cancer, but ulcerative colitis has a much higher risk than Crohn's.

D. There are strong positive associations with tobacco smoking, high animal fat consumption, and other lifestyle risk factors which appear to increase the risk of developing colon cancer. These associations are not as well correlated as the known risks of adenomatous polyps, IBD, and familial polyposis syndromes.

E. Familial polyposis syndromes are a result of a defect of the adenomatous polyposis coli gene on the long arm of chromosome 5. People with this defect develop adenomas early in the second decade of life and have hundreds and even thousands of adenomatous polyps with an extremely high risk of cancer by the age of 40. The illustration shows a familial polyposis case that resulted in colon carcinoma fatality in a 20-year-old girl.

ANSWER 45

C. Squamous cell cancers of the lung, head and neck, and esophagus are known to produce a protein that is similar, but not identical, to parathyroid hormone. This parathyroid hormone-related polypeptide results in hypercalcemia which can be severe and life-threatening. The symptoms of hypercalcemia are abdominal pain, nausea, vomiting, constipation, polyuria, confusion, and stupor. A serum calcium (and albumin, to allow for correction) or an ionized calcium should be obtained on all patients with a history of squamous cell carcinoma who present with mental status changes.

A. Lambert–Eaton (LE) syndrome occurs with small cell lung cancer and is characterized by weakness, myalgias, and fatigability. A key feature that distinguishes Lambert–Eaton syndrome from myasthenia gravis is that muscle strength *improves* with repeated stimulation in LE syndrome and it *fatigues* with repeat stimulation in MG. The primary defect in LE syndrome is impaired release of the neurotransmitter acetylcholine from the presynaptic nerve terminal.

B. Ectopic erthropoietin production has been described in renal cell carcinomas, hepatomas, and cerebellar hemangiomas. This results in a relative polycythemia.

D. Excess ADH production is associated with small cell lung cancers (as opposed to squamous cell cancer's association with hypercalcemia) and results in hyponatremia and hypoosmolarity. When distinguishing SIADH from other causes of hyponatremia, a critical feature of SIADH is an abnormally concentrated urine (>300 mOsm/kg) in the setting of hyponatremia and hypoosmolality.

E. Ectopic ACTH production is associated with small cell lung cancer, carcinoid tumors, and thyroid cancers. This ectopic ACTH can result in Cushing's syndrome. Clinically apparent Cushing's syndrome is estimated to occur in 5% of patients with small cell lung cancer.

ANSWER 46

B. This patient has acute epididymitis, most commonly caused by *Chlamydia trachomatis* in a young adult patient, but gonorrhea is a possible etiology. Treatment is with IM Ceftriaxone and oral Doxycycline to cover both pathogens. In older patients, the etiology is more commonly gram-negative organisms like those seen in the GI tract. The increased blood flow is due to the inflammation of the left epididymis.

A. Although testicular cancer is a disease mainly affecting young men, it is generally painless and not associated with fever.

C. Testicular torsion is in the differential diagnosis of any teen or young adult male presenting with acute scrotal pain. However, the pain is usually worse with elevation of the scrotum, and the cremasteric reflex is frequently absent. Also, the radionucleotide scan showing adequate blood flow to the left testis rules out this diagnosis.

D. The leukocyte esterase in this patient's urine is due to the asymptomatic urethritis that is commonly seen with epididymitis. His picture is classic for epididymitis, and he has no other symptoms of a UTI.

E. This patient has no other signs or symptoms consistent with mumps.

ANSWER 47

C. This patient has psychogenic polydipsia related to her psychiatric disease. These patients may drink huge amounts of water a day. Their normal body physiology tries to get rid of the excess free water, but the intake is too much for their kidneys to excrete. The serum osmolality is low, the patient appears euvolemic on exam, and the urine is appropriately very dilute, as the kidneys are trying hard to excrete as much free water as possible.

A. When evaluating hyponatremia, the first test to order is the serum osmolality. If the osmolality is normal, the hyponatremia may be "pseudohyponatremia" which is a laboratory artifact due to extremely elevated serum proteins or lipids. With recent testing procedures, this artifact has been virtually eliminated. This patient has low serum osmolality.

B. Diabetes insipidus is central or nephrogenic. In central diabetes insipidus, there is a lack of ADH (antidiuretic hormone) produced by the posterior pituitary. In nephrogenic diabetes insipidus, the kidneys do not respond to the normal amount of ADH that is released. Diabetes insipidus causes a hypernatremia only if patients are unable to drink enough water to replace the free water they lose in their urine. These patients do *not* have a low serum osmolality but may have a normal or high serum osmolality with an inappropriately dilute urine.

D. SIADH (or Syndrome of Inappropriate Antidiuretic Hormone) presents with hyponatremia, hypoosmolarity of the serum (too much ADH is being secreted, often by an ectopic source), euvolemia, and a urine that is *inappropriately* concentrated for the degree of serum osmolality. Our patient has appropriately dilute urine for her degree of serum osmolality.

ANSWER 48

B. This patient has non-worrisome low back pain without neurologic symptoms or other "red flags." He is older than 20 years and younger than 50 years with no history of trauma. Back pain has been present for less than 6 weeks. His pain is most likely related to deconditioning and obesity putting strain on the low back. Physical therapy will often be helpful by improving strength and flexibility of the muscles in the lower back. Alternatively, such exercises could simply be taught in the office.

A. Because he is between 20 and 50 years with no history of trauma or malignancy and no neurologic findings on exam, this patient does not need to have any imaging of his spine until the pain has been present for 6 weeks.

C. Bed rest for more than 1–3 days can lead to deconditioning and worse back pain.

D. Most patients do not require narcotic use in benign low back pain. This patient's pain should be managed with nonsteroidal anti-inflammatory drugs.

E. MRI of the spine is also unnecessary in this setting of "benign" back pain that has been present for only 2 weeks. Most non-worrisome back pain will resolve within 4–6 weeks.

ANSWER 49

C. Patients with lone atrial fibrillation have a low risk (<1% per year) of thromboembolism and do not need chronic anticoagulation. Lone atrial fibrillation is a rare condition. A diagnosis of lone atrial fibrillation can only be made in patients younger than 60 without structural heart disease or other non-valvular risk factors for thromboembolism, such as hypertension, CHF, LV dysfunction, enlarged atrium, or prior thromboembolism.

A. Atrial fibrillation gets more prevalent with each decade of life.

B. Warfarin is more effective than aspirin at preventing thromboembolism in atrial fibrillation patients.

D. The risk for thromboembolism continues for weeks after cardioversion, as the atrium regains contractility. Anticoagulation should be continued for 4 weeks after cardioversion.

E. A patient with this scenario should be cardioverted electrically immediately.

ANSWER 50

E. A suppressed TSH level would imply a hyperfunctioning or "hof" nodule is present. These nodules are less likely to be malignant than cold nodules.

A–D are all associated with a higher likelihood that a dominant nodule will be malignant and should push the clinician towards a more aggressive approach to diagnosis, usually starting with FNAB (fine needle aspiration and biopsy). A hard nodule fixed to the skin, lymphadenopathy, or systemic signs of cancer would be other obvious clues to a more malignant origin of the thyroid nodule.

Q&A

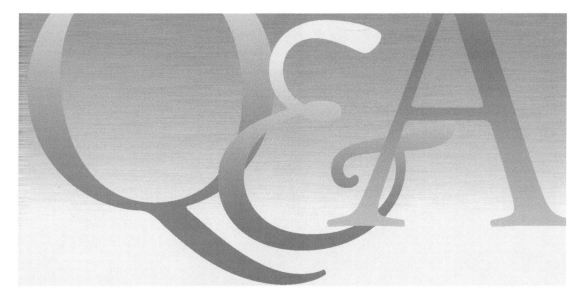

BLOCK TWO

ANSWERS

ANSWER 51

E. This patient has been infected with tuberculosis, but he has not developed pulmonary tuberculosis. Appropriate prophylaxis is 6–9 months of isoniazid therapy.

A. Two drugs are unnecessary for prophylaxis.

B. There is no need to send sputum if there are no radiographic lung findings.

C. This would be the appropriate therapy in the setting of lung infection with positive chest x-ray and sputum findings. However, the CXR shown is normal.

D. This PPD is positive because it is greater than 15 mm of induration. (Even 10 mm is considered positive in a health care worker who has likely been exposed to a patient with TB.)

ANSWER 52

A. This lady is presenting with a classic case of primary biliary cirrhosis (PBC). Most patients with PBC are women in the age range of 30–60 years. Many cases are asymptomatic and picked up incidentally when an elevated alkaline phosphatase is noted on labs. When patients become symptomatic, they may complain of pruritis. Often they complain of fatigue. Many patients will have evidence of other autoimmune disease such as Raynaud's disease, sicca syndrome, CREST syndrome or thyroid disease. The anti-mitochondrial antibody is very specific and sensitive for PBC.

B. This patient has fatigue, which could go along with hypothyroidism, and pruritis, which is sometimes seen in hyperthyroidism; however, the isolated alkaline phosphatase elevation and her symptoms should make you think of PBC. The best way to diagnose PBC is by ordering an AMA.

C. A sedimentation rate is a marker of inflammation. It is very nonspecific and would not help you diagnose PBC.

D. Alpha-I antitrypsin deficiency does not manifest with isolated elevated alkaline phosphatase and these symptoms. It should be considered when there is asymptomatic elevation of hepatic transaminases or in cirrhosis of unclear etiology.

E. Ceruloplasmin is the carrier protein for copper. The level is reduced in Wilson's disease which is a disorder of copper metabolism and clearance. Copper deposits occur in the liver, CNS, and Decemet's membrane of the cornea forming Kayser–Fleisher rings. In adults, the disease usually presents with CNS symptoms such as psychiatric illness and bizarre behavior. There may also be transaminase elevation.

ANSWER 53

C. Tumor lysis syndrome occurs usually at the onset of chemotherapy in the setting of rapidly proliferating malignancies such as high grade lymphomas or acute leukemias. Tumor lysis syndrome causes rapid and severe metabolic changes, including hyperkalemia, hyperphosphatemia, hypocalcemia, and hyperuricemia. End-organ damage may occur from uric acid crystals or calcium phosphate crystals precipitating in the renal tubules. Hypocalcemia is caused by the precipitation of calcium phosphate. Hyperkalemia can cause cardiac rhythm disturbances and/or death.

Treatment of tumor lysis syndrome begins with identifying the patient at risk and preventing the metabolic and end-organ changes. Hyperkalemia must be treated aggressively with Kay-exalate. Avoidance of uric acid crystals depositing in the kidney is done by alkalinizing the urine with sodium bicarb and maintaining high urine outputs. Acetazolamide may help with the urinary alkalinization, and allopurinal may be given which inhibits xanthine oxidase and the production of uric acid.

ANSWER 54

D. This patient's painful, vesicular rash that is limited to only one dermatome is consistent with herpes zoster, a reactivation of latent varicella zoster virus.

A. This would be a very unusual location and presentation of herpes simplex, which more commonly causes vesicles on mucous membranes of the mouth and genital area.

B. Eczema is generally pruritic, not painful. It is not usually vesicular.

C. Cellulitis does not cause a vesicular rash like this; it is more likely to cause localized swelling, warmth, and erythema.

E. Tinea is a fungal infection of the skin which generally causes ring-shaped lesions, and it is pruritic rather than painful.

ANSWER 55

D. In a patient with acute renal failure, urine electrolytes can serve as an indicator of the functional integrity of the renal tubules. This is done by calculating the fractional excretion of sodium (FENA). The calculation is most helpful in the setting of acute, olig-uric renal failure. (It is less helpful in other settings of renal failure and when patients are on diuretics.) It helps to differentiate between prerenal causes of acute renal fail-ure and intrarenal causes of acute renal failure.

The FENA is expressed as a percentage and is calculated by the following equation:

$$\text{Urine [Nal]/Plasma [Na]/Urine [Cr]/Plasma [Cr]} \times 100.$$

A FENA of less than 1% suggests that the kidney tubules are functioning to retain sodium and water appropriately, as they are sensing a lack of perfusion (prerenal problems). Causes of acute renal failure due to prerenal causes with a FENA <1% are cardiogenic shock, severe volume deple-tion, and radiocontrast nephropathy. Radiocon-trast nephropathy causes a "prerenal picture" by the FENA <1% because it causes spasming of the afferent arterioles. In renal failure secondary to acute tubular necrosis (ATN), the kidney tubules are broken and cannot resorb and avidly hold water and sodium, so the FENA is *high* (or greater than 1%).

ANSWER 56

A. This patient has Takayasu's arteritis, a vas-culitis affecting mainly the aorta and its major branches. It is most common in young women, and it can involve hyperten-sion from renal artery stenosis and aortic regurgitation from aortitis. Diminished or absent pulses is a classic sign of this dis-ease. Generalized fatigue is also common, and other systemic signs like fevers and ele-vated ESR can also be seen.

B. Although glomerulonephritis can cause hypertension, it should include blood and often RBC casts on urinalysis.

C. Essential hypertension is a diagnosis of exclusion. This patient has too many sec-ondary signs to diagnose essential hyper-tension, including a heart murmur and diminished pulses.

D. Despite this patient's heart murmur, there are no peripheral stigmata of SBE (like Janeway lesions, Osler's nodes, splinter hemorrhages, and Roth spots) and no fever. Furthermore, endocarditis does not cause hypertension.

E. Buerger's disease is a disease of peripheral vascular insufficiency seen in smokers. This is a disease of small vessels and would not cause aortic insufficiency.

ANSWER 57

B. Both have been found to improve clinical outcomes and reduce mortality after infarction. Beta-blockers are most effective in high risk patients with impaired LV function and ventricular arrhythmias. ACE inhibitors decrease mortality after anterior MI and depressed left ventricular function, presumably by inhibiting infarct remodeling.

A. Although frequent VPCs are a risk factor for sudden death in patients with heart abnormalities, routine treatment does not improve mortality and may well be harmful.

C. Neither nitrates, nor calcium channel blockers improve mortality in this setting. Diltiazein may prevent re-infarction in the setting of non-Q-wave infarction, but routine use of calcium channel blockers in other infarctions is not first line therapy and may be harmful.

D. Coronary angiography should be undertaken for postinfarction angina or if results of a rehabilitation stress test are positive. Many cardiologists also routinely catheterize non-Q-wave infarctions because of a high reinfarction rate, though the benefit of this approach remains controversial.

E. Aspirin reduces recurrent infarction by 30% and late mortality by 15%, and should be routinely given post infarct.

ANSWER 58

E. This patient presents with symptoms of pituitary dysfunction. In general, the trophic hormone levels such as TSH, GH, LH, FSH, and ACTH would be expected to be low.

A. Note that she has no goiter with a pituitary cause of hypothyroidism. Both TSH and T4 would be low in the setting of pituitary induced hypothyroidism.

B. Primary ovarian failure would lead to the profile shown in answer B. With a pituitary source of amenorrhea, you should see a low estradiol and a low LH/FSH.

C. Insulin-like growth factor is secreted by the liver and other tissues in response to GHRH. Growth hormone deficiency is common manifestation of hypopituitarism, and the levels of insulin-like growth factor would be decreased. Clinical signs of GH deficiency include hyponatremia, asthenia, obesity, and muscle weakness.

D. A patient with a pituitary source of a low cortisol state would have an inappropriately low ACTH level in addition to an abnormal cosyntropin stimulation test. This patient would also be expected to have adrenal responsiveness to prolonged exogenous ACTH stimulation. Note that the hyperkalemia, hyperpigmentation, and orthostasis characteristic of mineralocorticoid deficiency are not present in this patient. These signs are often more prominent in primary adrenocortical failure (Addison's disease).

The source of hypopituitarism would need to be defined and the appropriate hormonal replacement therapy given. She may have had pituitary hemorrhage with her last delivery and, in fact, may now have empty sella syndrome. In cases like this one, when there is a combined ACTH/TSH deficiency, glucocorticoid therapy should be initiated prior to thyroid hormone replacement to avoid precipitation of an adrenal crisis.

ANSWER 59

A. This patient has pulmonary tuberculosis with classic symptoms, positive PPD, positive chest x-ray and positive sputum. He should be started on four-drug therapy. After 2 months, therapy can be changed to just isoniazid and rifampin if the organism is susceptible to both of these drugs. Therapy should be continued for a total of 6 months.

B. This patient has pulmonary tuberculosis, so prophylaxis with isoniazid is inadequate therapy.

C. Mycobacterium tuberculum cultures can take several weeks to grow, so it is necessary to begin therapy before culture results are available.

D. Nearly all patients should be started on 4-drug therapy, but drugs can be adjusted after 2 months depending on culture sensitivity results.

E. This patient is in a high risk group, so an induration of 10 mm or more is considered positive.

ANSWER 60

B. A Schatzki's ring is a congenital web-like constriction in the distal esophagus at the squamocolumnar junction. It produces dysphagia when the lumen diameter is less than 13 mm. Patients have a history of dysphagia to solids that is intermittent and may extend back into childhood. It is unrelated to GERD.

A. Peptic strictures occur in approximately 10% of patients with reflux esophagitis. Short peptic strictures are usually 1–3 cm long and are present in the distal esophagus near the squamocolumnar junction. Patients with peptic strictures usually have a history of GERD and complain of dysphagia to solid foods.

C. Barrett's esophagus is a replacement of the squamous epithelium of the esophagus by columnar epithelium (also called "intestinal metaplasia"). It is a precancerous change, and adenocarcinoma occurs in 2–5% of cases of Barrett's.

D. Erosive esophagitis is a complication of GERD and involves endoscopically visible damage to the mucosa. The mucosa appears red and friable and has superficial linear ulcers which may bleed. There also may be exudates seen.

E. The incidence of adenocarcinoma of the esophagus is on the rise. It is more common in white patients than in blacks and in patients who have had a history of chronic GERD and Barrett's esophagus.

ANSWER 61

E. Seventy to eighty percent of women with breast cancer do *not* have an identifiable risk factor. For this reason, mammography screening has been used and has been shown to reduce mortality in women aged 50–74 years when done regularly. The current recommendation is annual screening exams.

ANSWER 62

B. This patient has pelvic inflammatory disease, a sexually transmitted infection of the endometrium, Fallopian tubes, and pelvic peritoneum. Clues to the diagnosis include cervical motion tenderness, cervical discharge, and fever. The most common causative organisms are *Neisseria gonorrhoeae* and *Chlamydia trachomatis*. A patient with the above symptoms should be treated for both organisms, since both organisms may commonly be seen co-infecting the same patient.

A. A UTI might cause fevers and suprapubic tenderness but should not cause cervical motion tenderness or a cervical discharge.

C. Toxic shock syndrome, caused by the exotoxin from Staph or Strep infection, results in a septic shock picture with a rash, hypotension, and end-organ failure.

D. Bacterial vaginosis is an inflammation of the vagina and cervix caused most commonly by *Gardnerella vaginalis*. Symptoms include vaginal discharge with a "fishy" odor. The disease has not been proven to be sexually transmitted. It does not cause cervical motion tenderness or fevers.

E. *Trichomonis vaginalis* is sexually transmitted and causes a purulent vaginal discharge and vulvar irritation with inflammation and sometimes petechial lesions on the cervix ("strawberry cervix"). However, it does not cause cervical motion tenderness or fevers.

ANSWER 63

B. Neoplasms of the urinary tract account for 15–20% of cases of patients with hematuria after the age of 40, and two-thirds of these are carcinomas of the bladder.

Hematuria is greater than 4 RBCs per high power field. Normal individuals may excrete as many as 10^4 RBCs in the urine during a 12-hr period. Among adults over 35 years of age, the prevalence of microhematuria was found to be 13%. The causes of hematuria are age dependent. Glomerular causes predominate in children and young adults, and neoplasms of the urinary tract account for 15–20% of patients with hematuria over the age of 40. Urinary calculi and urinary tract infections are also common causes of hematuria in adults. Persistent microhematuria with episodic gross hematuria as well as deformed red cells and red cell casts seen on the microscopic analysis all support a glomerular source of bleeding. Patients with intermittent or continuous asymptomatic microhematuria or episodic gross hematuria with complete clearing of the urine between episodes suggests extrarenal pathology. Urine dip testing is sensitive but not specific for hematuria. The test also picks up myoglobin pigment and free hemoglobin pigment and calls it "positive" for blood. Therefore, urine dip tests that are positive for blood should be followed with a microscopic urinalysis.

ANSWER 64

D. This patient has Wegener's granulomatosis. This is an inflammatory, necrotic granulomatous disease that mainly involves the lungs, kidneys, and upper respiratory tract (including sinusitis and glomerulonephritis). It does not include hilar adenopathy on chest x-ray. Antineutrophil cytoplasmic antibody is a classic marker supportive of the diagnosis of WG. However, it is not diagnostic because it can be seen with several other autoimmune diseases. Diagnosis is made by biopsy of the lung, nose, or sinuses.

A. Although Goodpasture's syndrome also involves both lungs and kidney, it is characterized by antibasement membrane antibody, not ANCA. It does not typically involve sinusitis. The clinical picture is typically one of hemoptysis, microscopic hematuria, and abnormal renal function.

B. Polyarteritis nodosa is a vasculitis that commonly affects multiple organ systems, including the kidneys. However, it also frequently involves skin and GI tract, and it does not cause granulomas in the lungs. A positive ANCA is not consistent with this diagnosis.

C. Although SLE commonly involves the kidneys, the lung findings are classically pleuritic inflammation, not granulomas. Also, 90% of lupus patients have a positive ANA, and very few have a positive ANCA.

E. Although sarcoidosis does cause granulomas in the lungs and fatigue, it does not cause renal involvement; nor does it cause a positive antineutrophil cytoplasmic antibody.

ANSWER 65

D. ACE inhibitors improve symptoms, improve cardiac output and improve survival in patients with diminished LV function. They are started at a low dose and titrated up as the BP and other potential side effects of cough, hyperkalemia, and renal insufficiency allow.

A. Digoxin may improve symptoms and reduce hospitalizations in patients with CHF, but does not improve mortality. It is most useful for patients with an S3 or atrial fibrillation.

B. Furosemide dramatically improves symptoms of fluid overload but does not improve mortality.

C. Nitrates do not improve mortality in and of themselves. In CBF patients unable to tolerate ACE Inhibitors, high dose hydralazine and nitrates in combination have had a favorable effect on mortality, though reaching the therapeutic dosage range of this combination is often difficult.

E. Dobutamine can be used short term for severe refractory CHF symptoms, but may actually accelerate mortality.

ANSWER 66

D. Demeclocycline can induce diabetes insipidus and can be used to treat SIADH if water restriction alone is unsuccessful. Hypotonic saline solutions could make the hyponatremia of SIADH worse, and the other agents can cause SIADH. Desmopressin is a vasopressin analogue used to treat diabetes insipidus. Chlorpropamide is an oral hypoglycemic associated with SIADH. Carbemazepine (Tegretol) is an antiepileptic that can induce SIADH and may be used to treat milder forms of Diabetes insipidus. Vincristine, vinblastine, tricyclic antidepressants, pain, nausea, malignancies, pulmonary, and neurological conditions are also associated with SIADH.

ANSWER 67

B. This patient's symptoms and physical findings are consistent with gradual worsening of his COPD. Spirometry can guide medical management by evaluating the severity of the patient's functional airway obstruction. The FEV_1 is also helpful in predicting mortality in patients with COPD.

A. This patient has no change in sputum, fevers, or other signs of infection. He is functionally at baseline, so there is no reason to treat with antibiotics. Furthermore, if he were having an infection of the respiratory tract, erythromycin would be inadequate coverage in this elderly man with COPD.

C. A cough suppressant would not treat this patient's underlying disease, which is his COPD. Re-evaluation of his medical regimen of bronchodilators and theophylline with appropriate dose adjustments and consideration of inhaled steroids or long-term bronchodilators would be more appropriate management.

D. Because the patient's symptoms are consistent with his COPD, further workup is unnecessary. The weight loss is most likely attributable to the COPD, and he has no lesions on chest x-ray suggestive of malignancy.

E. This patient is not sufficiently hypoxic to qualify for home oxygen therapy. He would need a PO_2 of 55 or less to warrant such therapy. Other criteria for long-term home oxygen therapy in COPD includes a PO_2 of 56–59 with cor pulmonale or erythrocytosis. Oxygen can be prescribed for use during exercise or sleep if the PO_2 goes down to 55 or less with exercise or sleep.

ANSWER 68

B. Patients with gastric ulcers have *normal* or *decreased* gastric acid secretion, and patients with duodenal ulcers have increased gastric acid secretion.

A. *Helicobacter* infection is associated with *both* duodenal and gastric ulcer disease, but *more* duodenal ulcers are associated with *H. pylori* infection than gastric ulcers.

C. In a classic presentation of DU and GU, patients with DU tend to have relief of pain with eating, and patients with GU have worsening of their pain with eating.

D. NSAIDs cause more gastric ulcers than duodenal ulcers.

E. Gastric ulcers are slower to heal than duodenal ulcers, and there is more of a risk of malignancy with a gastric ulcer that hasn't healed. Therefore, many gastroenterologists will repeat endoscopy on patients in 2 months to assess the healing process and to take biopsies if malignancy is suspected.

ANSWER 69

E. Goodpasture's syndrome is a collagen vascular disorder that involves pulmonary hemorrhage and glomerulonephritis secondary to anti-basement membrane antibodies in the kidneys and lungs. Diffuse bilateral pulmonary infiltrates are usually seen. The hemoptysis may be severe enough to cause anemia.

A. Wegener's is a vasculitis that also has pulmonary and renal involvement, but it does not have anti-basement membrane antibodies. It is classically seen with anti-neutrophil cytoplasmic antibodies in the serum.

B. Although lupus can involve both the kidneys and the lungs, it also is not associated with anti-BM antibodies. It is more commonly seen with positive ANA and other specific serum antibodies.

C. Hemophilia B, or congenital factor IX deficiency, can cause a variety of bleeding problems, including hemarthrosis and post-surgical bleeding. Hemophilia B does not have antibodies to the basement membrane.

D. The urinalysis findings are consistent with a glomerulonephritis, but this does not account for the hemoptysis or for the anti-BM antibodies.

ANSWER 70

D. This patient has Lyme disease, a tick-borne, spirochetal illness that has three clinical stages. The first stage includes flu-like symptoms, and 50% of patients have the classic rash of erythema chronicum migrans, an expanding erythematous area with central clearing. The second stage, which occurs weeks to months later, can include arthritis of the large joints and neurologic symptoms, including a Bell's palsy. Cardiac symptoms, including heart block, can also be seen in Stage 2.

A. Cerebrovascular accidents without underlying cause are unusual in such young patients. Also, it would be rare for a left-sided cerebrovascular accident to cause only unilateral facial nerve weakness. Furthermore, if the lesion were central, the muscles of the forehead would be spared. This patient's problem is a lesion of the peripheral cranial nerve VII, also called Bell's palsy, which is frequently seen in Lyme disease. The knee inflammation would also not be seen with a CVA.

B. Erythema multiforme is a rash, often drug-induced, which includes multiple skin lesions of various shapes and sizes. The classic lesion is the "target lesion." Mucous membranes can also be involved. However, the rash pictured is that of erythema chronicum migrans.

C. Myasthenia gravis, a disease of the neuromuscular junction, can cause weakness, including facial weakness. However, the weakness is not generally strictly unilateral, and it more commonly involves the extraocular and eyelid muscles. It would not cause an inflammatory arthritis.

E. A post-viral syndrome, although it could cause an arthritis, would have been unlikely to cause the original "donut-shaped" rash of erythema migrans.

ANSWER 71

A. This patient is presenting with fluid overload and EKG signs of hyperkalemia because of her lack of renal dialysis. She should be placed on oxygen and given calcium IV to stabilize the cardiac membrane. Hyperkalemia predisposes patients to ventricular arrythmias with possibilities of cardiac arrest and death. The initial signs of hyperkalemia seen on the EKG include peaked pointed T waves (as seen in the figure). You must know the other EKG signs of hyperkalemia, however, because peaked T waves are only seen in 22% of patients with hyperkalemia. As potassium levels increase, the P wave decreases in amplitude and increases in duration. The PR interval prolongs, reflecting AV node conduction delay. More severe hyperkalemia induces complete flattening of the P wave and widening of the QRS. A pattern resembling RBBB, LBBB, or nonspecific intraventricular conduction delay may develop. If hyperkalemia remains untreated, sine waves, AV block, or ventricular fibrillation occurs.

The treatments include:

1) *Stabilize* the cardiac membrane with calcium

2) *Shift* the potassium out of the circulation and into the cell with albuterol or B-adrenergic agonists, glucose and insulin, or bicarbonate

3) *Remove* the potassium from the body with sodium polystyrene or lasix.

ANSWER 72

A. This patient has polyarteritis nodosa with classic physical findings of this vasculitis including palpable purpura, livedo reticularis, mononeuritis multiplex, and kidney involvement. Hypertension is seen in 50% of the patients with renal involvement. Polyarteritis nodosa is frequently seen in the presence of chronic hepatitis B, which this patient likely has as a result of his IV drug use.

B. Although Henoch–Schonlein purpura does cause a purpuric rash, this rash is generally on the lower extremities and buttocks. Renal involvement is not uncommon with HSP, but it does not generally cause peripheral nerve involvement. The abdominal involvement is generally more diffuse secondary to vascular insufficiency of the GI tract not limited to the right upper quadrant.

C. ITP can cause a purpuric-type rash not merely petechiae. ITP is a diagnosis of exclusion, and the multiple additional symptoms argue against this diagnosis.

D. This patient definitely does have liver disease, which can cause a decrease in production of coagulation factors, resulting in bleeding complications. However, purpura is usually the result of platelet deficiency or vasculitis not coagulation factor deficiencies. Also, this would not explain the peripheral nerve or kidney involvement.

E. Despite his IV drug use, this patient does not have HIV. Therefore, Kaposi's sarcoma is unlikely.

ANSWER 73

C. CHF has a substantial mortality rate, with the most common causes of death being progressive heart failure, sudden death due to ventricular arrhythmias, stroke, and related coronary artery disease. ACE Inhibitors are the mainstay of treatment. They decrease afterload and reduce sodium retention by inhibition of aldosterone secretion. They reduce the progression to clinical CHF in those with asymptomatic LV dysfunction, reduce hospitalization, and reduce mortality in those with moderate to severe CHF. Carvedilol and other beta-blockers also reduce mortality rates, probably by reducing ventricular arrhythmias (Carvedilol also has afterload reduction properties). Beta-blockers must be used with caution in any patient with CHF by carefully watching clinical response as the dose is titrated upward. They should be started only if the patient has already tolerated therapeutic doses of an ACE inhibitor. Recent trials have shown mortality reduction with Aldactone in patients with moderate to severe CHF.

A. Neither digoxin nor furosemide reduces mortality.

B. Coumadin may improve outcomes in those with CHF. It has established benefit in those with atrial fibrillation or LV thrombus and CHF, and is commonly used in those who have very low ejection fractions even without those comorbidities. Digoxin does not confer mortality benefit.

D. Dobutamine may increase mortality, though it can be useful for severe refractory CHF symptom relief.

E. Amlodipine is one of the only calcium channel blockers that has demonstrated safety in CHF if needed for angina or BP control, but does not reduce mortality. Hydralazine and nitrate combinations reduce mortality, but their use has largely been supplanted by the better-tolerated and more effective ACE inhibitors.

ANSWER 74

C. This patient is diagnosed at an advanced stage of primary adrenal insufficiency, also known as Addison's disease. The photo reveals hyperpigmentation of the skin and skin lines. This hyperpigmentation is indicative of increased ACTH and its MSH (melanocyte stimulating hormone) derivatives. The patient has signs of cortisol deficiency as well as aldosterone deficiency. Autoimmune adrenalitis, tuberculosis, and bilateral adrenal hemorrhage are some of the most common causes of primary adrenal insufficiency.

A. Aspirin overdose can cause acidosis but it is a positive anion gap acidosis. It can cause seizure activity, respiratory alkalosis, nausea, vomiting, hyperthermia, pulmonary edema, and death. It is not associated with hyperpigmentation and would be inconsistent with his longer history of changes over the last year.

B. Cushing's is associated with hyperglycemia, obesity, hypertension, etc.

D. Steroid withdrawal can cause adrenal insufficiency, but ACTH levels would be suppressed and there would be no hyperpigmentation. Steroid withdrawal is not associated with prominent aldosterone deficiency signs such as hyperkalemia and hyponatremia.

E. An elevated ACTH level as implied by the hyperpigmentation in this case would not be consistent with hypopituitarism. Hypopituitary origins of adrenal insufficiency would not be expected to produce the prominent signs of hypoaldosteronism (such as his electrolyte abnormalities).

ANSWER 75

D. This patient has classic symptoms of allergic rhinitis with "post-nasal drip." The seasonal nature of her symptoms further supports this diagnosis.

A. This patient has no fevers, and her cough is non-productive. Also, the itchy eyes and boggy nasal turbinates are more suggestive of allergic rhinitis than an infectious etiology.

B. A smoker's cough would be unlikely to be seasonal, and it would not account for her eye and nose findings.

C. Despite the mild sinus tenderness, this patient is more likely to have seasonal allergies causing her symptoms and causing some sinus fullness.

E. Chronic bronchitis involves a productive cough for at least 3 months of the year for at least two consecutive years. Furthermore, it generally is seen in older patients with a long smoking history.

ANSWER 76

E. The specific cause of hepatic encephalopathy is unknown, but the most important factors in the pathogenesis are severe hepatocellular dysfunction and/or intahepatic and extrahepatic shunting of portal venous blood into the systemic circulation so that the liver is bypassed. Because of these factors, toxic substances absorbed from the intestine are not detoxified by the liver and lead to metabolic abnormalities of the central nervous system. Ammonia is one of the toxic substances that accumulates, among many, and the serum marker that aids physicians in monitoring the patient's therapy.

In a patient with otherwise stable cirrhosis, hepatic encephalopathy usually follows a clear precipitating event. The most common predisposing event is gastrointestinal bleeding which leads to an increase in the production of ammonia and other nitrogenous substances that are then absorbed. Dehydration and hypokalemia with overuse of diuretics can precipitate encephalopathy because it causes an alkalemic state. In the alkalernic state, there is an increase in the amount of nonionic ammonia (NH_3) relative to the ammonium ions (NH_4^+). Nonionic ammonia crosses the blood-brain barrier and accumulates in the CSF. Hypokalemia also directly stimulates the kidneys to produce ammonia. Certain infections also may act as precipitating events to hepatic encephalopathy, and cirrhotic patients may not mount fever responses or white counts as readily as normal patients. SBP should be searched for as an etiology of hepatic encephalopathy in a known cirrhotic patient.

ANSWER 77

C. The hepatitis B vaccine induces the production of antibodies to Hep B surface antigen. Efficacy is greater than 90%. It involves a series of three injections. Recommended indications for administration of the vaccine include the following:
- All infants, regardless of mother's Hep B status
- All adolescents
- Household contacts of patients with hepatitis B, especially sexual contacts
- Patients with liver disease of other etiology, especially Hep C
- IV drug users and other individuals whose high risk behavior (e.g., sexual promiscuity) puts them at risk
- Health care workers
- Patients on chronic hemodialysis or who require repeated blood transfusions should be vaccinated. However, peritoneal dialysis is not an indication because it does not involve an increased risk of virus transmission.

A. Because Hep B is transmitted in blood and body fluids, IV drug users are a high risk population.

B. All infants should receive the Hep B vaccine. Infants of mothers whose HbsAg status is positive or unknown should receive the vaccine within 12 hr of birth.

D. Patients with liver disease of other etiology should be vaccinated against hepatitis A and B because such an infection could seriously complicate their underlying disease.

E. Adolescents should be vaccinated if they were not vaccinated as infants. The purpose of this "catch-up" vaccination program is to vaccinate all children before they reach adolescence when they are at potential risk of infection through sexual exposure and intravenous drug use.

ANSWER 78

C. The anion gap is calculated by the equation: $[Na + I - [(Cl-) + (HCO_3^-)]$

This calculation in our patient is: $[136] - [(109) + (16)] = 11$. A normal anion gap is 12 plus or minus 2; therefore, we would say that this is an acidosis (low bicarbonate) with a normal anion gap. You can see that the reason that the anion gap remained normal is because the chloride ion is increased. Therefore, the other name for this is a hyperchloremic non-anion gap acidosis.

You should instantly think of two main categories of disease that cause a hyperchloremic, non-anion gap acidosis. They are *renal* (specifically, renal tubular acidosis) and GI (usually diarrhea). Both of these disease categories have the *loss of bicarbonate* in common (causing the acidosis) and a retention of chloride ions.

The hyperkalemic types of distal RTA usually develop in patients with an underlying tubulointerstitial renal disease and/or those with moderate renal insufficiency who have aldosterone deficiency. This is particularly common in diabetics, especially those who have developed nephropathy. Hyperkalemia can be treated using exchange resins or lasix (if patients are volume overloaded) or mineralocorticoids if patients do not have problems with volume.

Patients who have protracted vomiting may develop a metabolic *alkalosis* because of the loss of hydrogen ions in the acidic fluid of the stomach and as a result of volume depletion.

ANSWER 79

C. This patient's exam and the high WBC count in his synovial fluid are consistent with a septic knee despite the negative gram stain. His use of chronic steroids for his RA put him at risk for infection. This patient needs to be admitted to the hospital for IV antibiotics.

A. Although an exacerbation of rheumatoid arthritis can cause significant synovitis and pain, it would not normally cause such a high WBC count in the synovial fluid.

B. Osteoarthritis does not give fevers and such significant synovial inflammation.

D. Felty's syndrome is rheumatoid arthritis together with neutropenia and splenomegaly.

E. There is no evidence that this patient had significant bleeding into his joint. The RBCs in the synovial fluid are most likely due to minor trauma at the time of the arthrocentesis.

ANSWER 80

A. As many as one-third of heart failure patients may have normal systolic function. Diastolic dysfunction is an abnormality of filling of the left ventricular cavity. The major components of diastole are ventricular relaxation, passive filling, and atrial contraction. The most common cause of diastolic dysfunction is LVH. Poor compliance of the ventricle requires higher pressures to fill the ventricle.

B. Dilated cardiomyopathy is ruled out by a normal echocardiogram.

C. Restrictive cardiomyopathy can also cause diastolic dysfunction, but the echo and history support the far more common condition of LVH as an etiology.

D. Coronary disease is much less likely in the absence of angina or EKG signs. Ischemia can cause transient diastolic or systolic dysfunction, but the echocardiogram and EKG are more supportive of LVH as an etiology.

E. Mitral stenosis can cause pulmonary edema but is not present on physical exam echocardiogram.

ANSWER 81

A. The patient has a Cushingoid appearance as manifest by his moon-like facies, centripetal obesity, striae, and possibly a buffalo hump. Diabetes and hypertension are very common problems in an outpatient setting, but the rapid onset of weight gain with his body habitus should make you suspicious of Cushing's syndrome. The first step is to confirm your impression of hypercortisolism. The best screening tests is the urinary free cortisol collection. The 1-mg overnight dexamethasone suppression test is another screening tool, but is less reliable than the urinary free cortisol test.

B. If you confirm the diagnosis of hypercortisolism, the next step is to determine if the hypercortisolism is ACTH dependent or not. An MRI scan would be appropriate if the ACTH level is high and suppressible with a high dose 8-mg dexamethasone suppression test, suggesting Cushing's disease as the source of his Cushing's syndrome.

C. This would be of secondary importance to confirming Cushing's syndrome. Hypothyroidism may be present but would not explain his hypertension, diabetes, or appearance.

D. This would ignore the probability that the patient has Cushing's syndrome.

E. ACTH levels may be relevant but are expensive and not appropriate for screening patients for Cushing's syndrome.

ANSWER 82

B. This patient has the restrictive lung pattern and decreased gas diffusion classic of interstitial lung disease. The fact that his symptoms improve when he is away from the farm suggests an occupationally related hypersensitivity pneumonitis. Farmer's lung is a hypersensitivity reaction to thermophilic actinomycetes.

A. This patient has no fever or productive cough, and the time course of his disease is with a community acquired pneumonia.

C. COPD has an obstructive pattern on pulmonary function tests.

D. Pulmonary coccidioidomycosis infection would not show this restrictive lung pattern. Symptoms would not abate when leaving the region, and the time course is wrong for acute pulmonary coccidioidomycosis.

E. Although CHF can cause a chronic cough and dyspnea, this patient has no findings on exam, like jugular venous distension or an S3, that would support this diagnosis.

ANSWER 83

C. The diagnosis of spontaneous bacterial peritonitis is made by careful examination of the ascites fluid and cultures that are performed at the bedside for greater sensitivity. A cell count of 500 white cells with 50% or greater polymorphonuclear cells (PMNs), or greater than 250 PMNs (*not* lymphocytes), makes the diagnosis of bacterial peritonitis.

Spontaneous bacterial peritonitis is an infection of the peritoneal cavity with bacteria that occurs without an obvious primary source of infection. Patients with end stage liver disease are particularly susceptible to this infection. The pathology seems to be transmigration of the enteric gram-negative bacteria through the bowel wall, transversing the lymphatics and into the blood stream. Because of the low content of albumin and opsonizing proteins in the ascites fluid, the fluid is predisposed to infection. The fluid is seeded with organisms by the hematogenous route. Enteric gram-negative bacilli are the causative agent in the majority of cases, and empiric treatment is a third-generation cephalosporin or ampicillin and an aminoglycoside. Patients with severe liver disease may not mount normal signs and symptoms of infection such as fever and elevated white counts; therefore, spontaneous bacterial peritonitis should be considered in a patient with liver disease and new onset of hepatic encephalopathy or worsening jaundice.

ANSWER 84

D. This patient has been on broad-spectrum antibiotics for a long time, so she is at risk for *Clostridium difficile*–induced diarrhea. This is a very common nosocomial infection, which presents clinically with watery diarrhea, lower abdominal pain, low grade fever and leukocytosis. Culture for *C. dif* is not adequate because it can be part of the normal flora. It is necessary to test for the presence of the *C. dif* toxin, which is the cause of the diarrhea.

A. As above, stool cultures will not give the answer of diarrhea induced by *C. difficile*. Furthermore, bacterial gastroenteritis frequently has blood or mucous in the stools.

B. The course of this patient's diarrhea is unlikely to have a parasitical etiology.

C. Colonoscopy would not be a good first test in a patient with only 1 day of diarrhea. The *C. dif* cytotoxin ELISA has a 70–90% sensitivity and 99% specificity, making colonoscopy a costly and unnecessary test.

E. This patient is unlikely to have a malabsorption as the primary cause of her diarrhea, so a fecal fat collection would not be a good initial test.

ANSWER 85

B. Acute renal failure is a relatively common medical problem. When evaluating the possible etiologies of renal failure in any given patient, it is helpful to categorize them as prerenal causes, intrarenal causes, and postrenal causes. Prerenal causes include anything that reduces blood flow to the kidneys, such as a low cardiac output, volume depletion, etc. Intrarenal causes include interstitial nephritis, glomerulonephritis, acute tubular necrosis, etc. Postrenal causes are caused by obstruction of the entire urinary tract. (Obstruction of just one ureter in a patient with two functional kidneys will not produce acute renal failure.) In a 70-year-old man, prostatic enlargement is a common cause of bladder outlet obstruction, and a quick intervention to do to a man who presents with renal failure is to place a foley catheter. The rest of the work up can continue after that.

ANSWER 86

D. Approximately half of the cases of antiphospholipid antibody syndrome are primary; most of the rest occur in association with SLE. These antibodies cause a prolonged PTT, inhibiting clotting in the test tube, but they are thrombogenic *in vivo*. Patients with this syndrome have an increased incidence of both venous and arterial blood clots. This patient has a history of venous clots, with a PE and DVT in the past. Now she presents with a CVA from arterial thrombosis. She needs lifelong anticoagulation with warfarin.

A. SLE can cause CNS involvement, most commonly psychosis or seizures. It would not generally cause the focal neurologic findings seen in this patient.

B. This patient does not have a fever or nuchal rigidity, so bacterial meningitis is unlikely. Also, meningitis rarely causes focal neurologic findings like unilateral weakness.

C. Uremic encephalopathy generally presents as mental status changes and confusion, not with focal motor findings.

E. Steroid psychosis can involve a variety of psychiatric symptoms, including hypomania and depression. Memory problems can also occur. However, focal motor findings are not seen in this condition.

ANSWER 87

E. A chest pain syndrome consistent with an acute coronary syndrome accompanied by a new left bundle branch block is an indication for the administration of lytics. The new left bundle branch block means this patient must be treated as an acute myocardial infarction, not as unstable angina. The new left bundle branch block would potentially obscure characteristic ST segment elevation. Lytics have been shown to reduce mortality and preserve LV function in acute MI. There may be benefit up to 24 hr after the onset of pain, but maximal benefit is achieved if lytics can be administered in the first several hours. Primary percutaneous transluminal angioplasty is at least as effective as lytics in this setting but is not immediately available in many settings.

A. The patient is having an acute MI. Failure to diagnose acute coronary syndromes is the number one cause of malpractice cases in the United States.

B. This patient should be admitted to the CCU after lytic administration. Heparin and beta-blockers on a telemetry unit may be appropriate for some unstable angina but are *not* appropriate as the sole therapy for an acute MI in a patient eligible for lytics or urgent PTCA.

C. Acute MI can mimic GI symptoms but H_2 blockers won't help an acute myocardial infarction.

D. An isolated left bundle branch block is not an indication for pacer placement. The patient needs to be monitored carefully for subsequent problems, however.

ANSWER 88

C. DM 2 has a very strong genetic tendency and twin concordance rates are almost 100%, compared to the 50% twin concordance rate in Type I DM.

A, B, D, and E are all true statements.

ANSWER 89

D. This patient has an exudative pleural effusion. She meets all three of Light's criteria with a fluid to serum protein ratio greater than 0.5, an LDH ratio greater than 0.6, and a total LDH more than two-thirds of the normal serum value. The effusion caused by CHF is generally transudative in nature.

A. A parapneumonic effusion is exudative. It may or may not have a positive gram stain. It will generally be high in WBCs. A pH of less than 7.1 means that the effusion is unlikely to resolve without chest tube drainage.

B. The pleural effusion seen with the pleurisy related to rheumatoid arthritis is usually exudative with a very low glucose.

C. Small cell lung cancer tends to metastasize early, so a malignant pleural effusion can be commonly seen. Such an effusion would be exudative and often has a low glucose, most often between 30 and 50.

E. Pulmonary tuberculosis involves a pleural effusion, which is exudative and usually has a relatively low glucose.

ANSWER 90

C. The stool osmotic gap is used to distinguish *osmotic* from *secretory* diarrhea (not inflammatory from secretary diarrhea). The osmotic gap is calculated by using the following formula: STOOL OSMOLALITY – 2(STOOL NA$^+$ + STOOL K$^+$) = OSMOTIC GAP. Stool osmolality is usually estimated using the measured plasma osmolality. An osmotic gap greater than 50 mOsmol/kg H$_2$O suggests an osmotic diarrhea.

A. On average, the normal adult produces about 150 g of stool a day. Diarrhea is defined as an increase in stool weight above 200 g a day, often with increased frequency and stool fluid content.

B. There are four pathophysiologic mechanisms that cause diarrhea: 1) increased secretion of electrolytes and water, such as in *V. cholera* infection, 2) osmotic diarrhea, such as caused by lactose intolerance, 3) inflammation, such as inflammatory bowel diseases, and 4) altered intestinal motility, leading to rapid transit times.

D. The D-xylose test is used in the evaluation of an osmotic diarrhea. It is helpful when checking for malabsorption syndromes and specifically measures the absorptive capacity of the proximal small bowel to absorb simple sugars. The definitive test for malabsorption due to intestinal mucosal disease is the small bowel biopsy.

ANSWER 91

E. This patient has classic findings of SBE, including a murmur consistent with mitral regurgitation, pulmonary congestion, weight loss, and peripheral stigmata from septic emboli (Janeway lesions and proteinuria). He most likely had a prior history of mitral valve prolapse, and his recent dental work puts him at risk for infection of that valve.

A. Urinary protein alone is insufficient to make the diagnosis of a UTI.

B. A pneumonia would not account for the heart murmur, weight loss, or Janeway lesions. His infiltrates are secondary to left-sided heart failure from an incompetent valve.

C. This patient is quite young for lung cancer secondary to smoking. Although it might account for the weight loss, it would not account for the heart murmur and is unlikely to account for the fevers. The x-ray findings also do not support a diagnosis of lung cancer.

D. Lymphoma could explain this patient's weight loss and chronic fevers, but it would not account for the other physical findings.

ANSWER 92

A. This patient has macroglossia, CHF with low voltage on EKG, carpal tunnel syndrome and symmetric arthritis. The most likely unifying diagnosis is amyloidosis. This can cause a restrictive cardiomyopathy with thickened ventricular walls because of amyloid deposition, resulting in low voltage EKG and CHF. It can also cause an arthritis, most often symmetric and involving the small joints, because of amyloid deposition in synovium and cartilage. Macroglossia and carpal tunnel syndrome are also commonly seen. Diagnosis is preferentially made by biopsy of the abdominal fat pad or rectum. With Congo Red staining, the amyloid will show apple-green birefringence under polarized light.

B. This finding would be diagnostic for gout. Uric acid crystals are needle-shaped and negatively birefringent gout would not account for the patient's CHF or macroglossia. It also does not commonly affect the small joint of the hands.

C. Anti-dsDNA antibodies are specific for systemic lupus erythematosis. Although SLE can cause arthritis and CHF symptoms (usually because of pericardial effusion), it would be unlikely to cause macroglossia or carpal tunnel syndrome.

D. This patient has no findings consistent with a cerebrovascular accident.

E. A pericardial effusion can cause CHF from tamponade and a low voltage EKG. However, this would not explain the arthritis, carpal tunnel syndrome, or macroglossia.

ANSWER 93

D. Adding aspirin to such a patient is the standard of care.

A. All mechanical valves in the aortic or mitral position require chronic anticoagulation.

B. The desired INR for mechanical valves is 2.5–3.5. A range of 2.0–3.0 is generally recommended for most other conditions.

D. The tissue valves don't last as long but are less thrombogenic compared to mechanical valves.

E. Life-long anticoagulation with an INR of 2.5–3.5 is needed for these valves with high thromboembolic potential.

ANSWER 94

E. This patient presents with severe hypercalcemia. Dehydration, lethargy, GI symptoms, renal insufficiency, and polydipsia/polyuria are all common features. The hypercalcemia is not PTH related, and the high calcium levels will suppress PTH. Non-specific treatment consists of vigorous hydration with normal saline followed by calciuresis induced by furosemide. Bisphosphonates are useful in all forms of severe hypercalcemia. Hypercalcemia associated with granulomatous disorders (such as sarcoid and TB) and lymphoma are caused by alpha1-hydroxlase that autonomously generates vitamin D-3 from vitamin D-2. Vitamin D dependent etiologies of hypercalcemia are generally responsive to steroids. Humoral hypercalcemia of malignancy could present an identical clinical picture but is not generally steroid responsive.

ANSWER 95

C. In a young nonsmoker with community acquired pneumonia, recommended empiric therapy is a macrolide, according to the American Thoracic Society and the Infectious Disease Society guidelines. This provides coverage for most community pathogens, including most *Streptococcus pneumoniae* and atypical organisms like mycoplasma.

A. If this patient had significant medical comorbidities or was over 60 years old, a beta-lactam with beta-lactamase inhibitor would be appropriate therapy. But it is not necessary in a young patient with an uncomplicated community acquired pneumonia.

B. There is no need for IV antibiotics in this patient with stable vital signs and adequate oxygenation. He can be treated with oral antibiotics as an outpatient.

D. As above, this patient does not require IV antibiotics. However, cefuroxime would be a good choice for a community acquired pneumonia that did require hospitalization.

E. Many sputum cultures give inadequate yield, and they can take several days to grow. It is, therefore, inappropriate to wait for culture results before starting empiric antibiotic therapy.

ANSWER 96

D. This patient has systemic lupus erythematosis. She has a malar rash, photosensitivity, arthritis, anemia, and nephropathy. She will likely also have a positive ANA. Antibody to double-stranded DNA is specific to SLE.

A. C-ANCA is seen in Wegener's granulomatosis and some other diseases. But it is not typically associated with SLE.

B. This patient has a systemic illness with associated arthritis. Her clinical picture is not consistent with a septic joint.

C. This patient's murmur sounds like a benign flow murmur. Although her fevers and proteinuria can be seen with endocarditis, this does not explain her malar rash, photosensitivity, or arthritis.

E. Complement levels may be decreased but not increased with an acute lupus flare.

ANSWER 97

E. The rhythm strip show a Mobitz I or Wenkebach second-degree AV nodal block. It is often associated with inferior wall infarctions. It requires no specific therapy unless there is hemodynamic compromise.

A. As above, this condition does not commonly lead to complete heart block.

B. The strip shows a Mobitz I type block, which is distinguished from a Mobitz II block by the progressive prolongation of the P-R interval before the nonconducted p wave appears.

C. No specific therapy is needed.

E. Blocked APCs are the most common cause of skipped beats on a tracing, but this is a Wenkebach block of the AV node.

ANSWER 98

B. This woman has been injecting her son's insulin, resulting in high insulin levels and hypoglycemia. Proinsulin is split at the C-peptide link to produce endogenous insulin; therefore, C-peptide is a reliable marker that rises with endogenous insulin secretion. A low C-peptide level with a high insulin level infers that the insulin is exogenous.

A. Insulinoma is a rare cause of hypoglycemia. The C-peptide level would be elevated along with the insulin level with insulinoma induced hypoglycemia.

C. Alcoholics can get hypoglycemic secondary to liver disease and loss of gluconeogenesis. This patient has hepatitis C, but her normal albumin and protein would argue against this mechanism, and the insulin level wouldn't be elevated.

D. The cortisol level would be low, but insulin levels would not be elevated with adrenal insufficiency. There are no other findings to suggest adrenal insufficiency.

E. Sulfonylureas are a common cause of hypoglycemia and this patient had access to them. Insulin levels may be high as the sulfonylureas enhance endogenous insulin secretion, but the C-peptide level would also be high, instead of decreased as in this case.

ANSWER 99

C. This patient is at risk for mesothelioma because of his history of asbestos exposure. Although it is a malignancy of the pleura, only about a quarter of patients with the diagnosis have positive pleural fluid cytology. However, the fluid is frequently bloody. The next step in the diagnostic work up would be a pleural biopsy, either thoracoscopic or via open thoracotomy. This will give the diagnosis 98% of the time.

A. This patient has no fever, cough, or other clinical signs of pneumonia.

B. The patient's PPD test was negative. A positive PPD test is based on induration not erythema. Pulmonary TB is, therefore, an unlikely diagnosis in this patient.

D. A malignant pleural effusion from small cell lung cancer almost always has positive cytology of the pleural fluid. Furthermore, small cell lung CA is rare in nonsmokers.

E. This patient has no evidence of infarct on EKG, and his effusion is exudative not transudative as would be expected in CHF.

ANSWER 100

B. Thrombotic thrombocytopenic purpura is a disorder characterized by a microangiopathic hemolytic anemia. It may occur as a result of pregnancy, AIDS, systemic lupus erythematosis, scleroderma, or Sjogren's syndrome, or for unknown reasons. Usually it is seen in young adults and in women more often than men.

The pathogenesis of the disorder starts with an injury to the arteriolar endothelium in localized arteriolar beds which activates platelets to form thrombi and causes fibrin deposition to occur. The red cells propelled through the vasculature by the force of blood flow are entrapped in the fibrin and sheared apart, forming schistocytes (fragmented red blood cells; see photo). These schistocytes are seen on the peripheral smear and are clues that something *physical* is shearing apart the red cells in circulation, creating an intravascular hemolytic anemia. This physical shearing property may be due to fibrin and platelets as in microangiopathic hemolytic anemia, or it may be an artificial heart valve. In any case, the hemolytic anemia is occurring by a nonimmune mediated events. Spherocytes are spherical red blood cells, which are usually caused by one of the two mechanisms. The first is hereditary spherocytosis, which is an autosomal dominant disorder of the red cell membrane which predisposes the cell to fragility and lysis. Another cause of spherocytes is an *immune*-related hemolysis, which is Coombs antibody positive. The cell gets a "bite" of membrane taken out as it passes through the spleen, causing a *lower* surface area to volume ration. The cell, then, becomes more spherical in shape. Therefore, *spherocytes* can be a marker of *immune*-related hemolytic anemia, but *schistocytes* are found in *non-immune* hemolytic anemia such as TTP.

The pentad of signs and symptoms found in TTP are:

1. Microangiopathic hemolytic anemia
2. Thrombocytopenia
3. Fever
4. Renal insufficiency
5. Neurologic problems such as decreased level of consciousness, confusion, and delirium